FINDING

THE

ELIXIR

To Hatcher,
Thank you for your support and
enthusiasm!! You know I'm a BIG
fan of yours and I'm proud of you!!
Enjoy your journey!!
With Gratitude!!
—Scott Looney

FINDING
THE
ELIXIR

HOW SPONTANEOUS TRAVEL
AND UNEXPECTED FRIENDSHIPS
HELPED RESET MY LIFE

SCOTT LOONEY

atmosphere press

For Mom & Roger, Dad,
and my brothers and sisters.

TABLE OF CONTENTS

INTRODUCTION

AUTHOR'S NOTE

When we're at our lowest points in life, thinking negatively, and seemingly without hope, new opportunities often present themselves right on time. Sometimes we just need the courage to step out of our comfort zone, have faith in humanity and explore. A dash of luck doesn't hurt either.

So how does a person meet amazing people, travel to incredible places and experience some of the greatest moments of their life after a painful divorce forced a complete shift in circumstances and priorities? The answers are in the following chapters. My hope is that you find these stories entertaining, meaningful and uplifting. They are all true.

HOW MY STORIES MIGHT HELP YOU

We all know life is about growth. After divorce, I allowed myself to "spread my wings" through travel and the experiences helped me learn and grow in significant ways. I traveled while happily married, but not enough for my taste. And after hearing from my wife that she was not happily married enough for her taste, I needed an escape. Not an escape toward denial, but an escape toward a place where I could look back on my 18-year relationship—and my life—and ask honestly, "What the hell happened?"

Use this book as a travel guide—one written for the journey of your heart and mind. May it bring you to much more than iconic landmarks along the way; may it also help you pursue and find the happiness we all truly deserve.

WHY TRAVEL?

We get one life to live on this planet. I have been incredibly fortunate to connect with new people and experience places I'd always imagined but didn't think I would ever really visit until much later. This was especially true while I was still picking up the pieces of my post-divorce life. I was trying to figure out where I would live, what I would do for a job/career and—most importantly—when I would be *happy* again. Traveling provides perspective which helped me heal, process the questions about the past and present, and feel less worried about the future.

So why am I telling my story through the lens of travel? It has to do with its most powerful metaphor. My hope is to be with someone I love above everything else at "the final travel destination" we all eventually reach. My best friend since sixth grade, Manny, sent me the following quote a few months after I told him about my divorce and the gut-wrenching feeling I had just wasted nearly two decades of my life.

"Your journey has molded you for the greater good.
It was exactly what it needed to be. Don't think you've
lost time. It took each and every situation you have

encountered to bring you to the now.
And now is right on time.”

- Asha Tyson

The quote is part irony, part metaphor and, perhaps, entirely how you'll feel after reading—or listening to—this book. My stories will hopefully entertain, inspire and add perspective to your life so you might enjoy the journey as much as possible before arriving at life's final destination.

THE OREGON COAST:

Tarot Cards and Tides

JOURNAL ENTRY (CIRCA 2014)

Prior to my first tarot card reading I had the misperception it was only practiced by gypsies and would provide a dangerous glimpse into my future. When I saw tarot card reading booths at local fairs, I thought the death card meant certain doom in the near future to said person. So when Jen promised she didn't consider herself a fortune teller, wouldn't charge me a dime, and just wanted to share her hobby with me, I told her I'd reconsider a reading. Looking back on the experience, I'm glad I reconsidered. The reading was refreshingly positive and gave me the opportunity to try something new when new things were happening in my life nearly every day.

And that's when I found myself on the Oregon Coast, leaving a proverbial message in a bottle for a woman I never planned on seeing again...

In the distant past, when people were distressed or "ill of mind" they would be sent to the countryside and to the ocean shores for rest and relaxation. And although some of those people likely needed more extensive help for whatever ailed them, there's a reason medical professionals of yesteryear saw the benefits of sending people away from cities and crowds of people. I'm happy to report fresh air therapy still works in the 21st century.

About five months after my divorce to my wife of 16 years, I took my first solo trip to the Oregon Coast. My world had been turned completely upside down, so I was in serious need of a fresh perspective. Over the years, my ex-wife and I had vacationed in many towns along the coast. By going back alone to the town we visited most often, I sought to prove to myself I could eventually be as happy going solo as I had been during all the trips we'd taken as a couple. I wanted to reclaim the coast as *mine* instead of ours.

We lived together for two years before being married for 16. So I'd spent the past several months eating and sleeping alone after rarely doing so throughout the previous 18 years. I still wasn't used to it. So was I a bitter divorcee then? Yes. I poured everything into our marriage and it wasn't enough.

"You're going back there alone?" This was the response of several people when explaining why I planned on driving to the same coastal city and hotel where my ex-wife and I had spent many vacations over the years.

"I need to prove I can do this." My reply served as an explanation to those who questioned my reasoning, but also to convince myself it would help me heal after my marriage ended.

As I made the nine-hour drive from my home heading west, the songs I listened to reminded me of all the years we had spent together. Some memories made me smile, while others had the opposite effect. At times I cried—and even sobbed—to the point of pulling over to the side of the road. I also stopped at some familiar places like Vista House that sits high above old Highway 30 at Crown Point State Scenic Corridor, east of Portland. We'd visited the location several times while taking driving breaks as a couple. On this trip, it gave me a chance to get out of my head for a moment and breathe. Looking out across the beautiful Columbia River provided some needed perspective—albeit temporarily. I knew the first trip alone would be difficult, but the drive over was excruciating. It was my own self-prescribed therapy, and I was no doctor. (Nor had I ever played one on TV.)

Predictably, when arriving on the chilly Oregon Coast I noticed some of the old familiar places we used to visit. The quaint shops we'd duck into when it rained—the antique stores with the little bells that ring whenever the door opens and closes—and local eateries we frequented in the past filled me with conflicting emotions. I would cycle through sadness, anger, frustration, loneliness and resolve. Throughout the stay, I questioned—more than once or twice—my decision to self-inflict so much pain and sorrow by taking a trip alone.

I even awoke in the middle of the night a time or two while having a conversation with her. It took me a moment to realize in the pitch dark I was the only one in the bed—and the room. The loneliness was unbearable at those times. Naturally, some parts of the trip were better without her, while other parts were not. So the words I'd been hearing from encouraging friends and family for months regarding this major life transition—"It'll get easier in the future"—started to make sense. Sometimes. Being reminded "when one door closes, another one opens" rang true—quite literally—when I visited some of the coastal antique and candy shops we'd spent time in over the years.

On the first Thursday of every month, the city's downtown shops and eateries stay open later and offer some things they don't normally provide on a daily basis. On Bannock Street, between 8th and 9th in Boise, The Chocolate Bar was a place we frequented and bought delicious Belgian chocolates on many of those first Thursdays. They often paired local wines with their amazing selection of chocolate goodies. On the same block, City Peanut Shop—with the same jingling bell in the door as the coastal shops—sold various packages of seasoned nuts and was another place we would drop into. Those were often Date Nights for us, and I always enjoyed them.

"I won't be going downtown for First Thursday for a while," I mentioned one night during that awkward time between being told she wanted a divorce and me moving out of our house a short time later.

"Why?" she asked.

"It'll remind me of all those times we went there together," I replied incredulously. "Those places and times have a special meaning for me."

"Those things always meant more to you than they did to me," she said unapologetically.

In retrospect, I realized she was already moving past what we'd shared as a couple for all those years. However, I was obviously not ready to fully process everything at that time. That comment remained with me much longer than expected and more than I ever showed. Time and place have always been meaningful to me. And, like many humans, I attach meanings and emotions to certain moments and memories. So I remain unapologetic in my appreciation of the times and places I've had the opportunity to experience with the special people in my life—both past and present.

Returning to the same beachfront hotel where we spent several vacations was intentional. The tears were not. Sitting at the end of the bed in a familiar room from the past triggered memories which were intended *and* unintended. Tears streamed down my face as I sat silently staring at the cloudy sky above the cold, gray Pacific Ocean from the windows of my room that afternoon. I remember wondering if she would feel sad on her first visit to the coast without me. She had been seeing a guy since before our divorce was finalized, so I doubted it. (Ouch.)

Rehashing our failed marriage to solve problems that were too late to be solved seemed a futile exercise to me, especially since I had already spent plenty of time on that topic in the months following the divorce. So I gathered myself and ventured onto the beach for the first time—completely alone. I had my phone and headphones but kept both in my pockets. Listening to the sound of the waves provides comfort every time I visit the coast. On that trip, especially, I needed to hear the ocean more than ever.

It was my first walk on the beach in nearly two decades without holding her hand, without smiling the knowing smiles all couples in love smile—especially on vacation when times are good. I caught myself reflecting on some of the good memories we'd made, and they made me smile. Nodding politely at happy couples walking by helped me realize I wasn't jaded after all. In a sense, I was going through a type of mourning. Our relationship had died. We had no children, so the likelihood of seeing each other was low. My life felt like it had been flipped upside down and sideways.

And it occurred to me I was now another statistic in the majority group of adults in the U.S. labeled as divorcees. But instead of jumping into a new relationship, I was about to do something more rare—I was taking a deep-dive look into myself. I truly believed that making new memories—and directly facing the old, painful ones—was the best way to move forward. (And I still believe that.) Even if that meant returning to all the old familiar places and remembering the times spent there together. Sometimes moving forward requires looking back—for a moment, anyway.

In the months following our divorce, I sought comfort and shelter from the storm. Sometimes that took the form of spending time with family and friends. Other times it meant

rinking lots of beer and mixed drinks while laughing and crying with family and friends—attempting to move on and forget
the past. Valiant strides were made on both fronts as I consumed personal-record quantities of alcohol and forged ahead
into my uncertain future. But ultimately, as humans, we really
can't forget the past, especially when the past has so recently
been the *present*. I knew that finding peace with my new normal was not going to happen overnight. But how long would
it take?

JEN AND ABBY

A few days before arriving on the coast, I'd connected with a
woman on a dating app. I wasn't looking for someone to date
or a serious relationship, but was missing and seeking female
companionship—in whatever form that took. We planned dinner at a great little Mexican food restaurant overlooking the
ocean for the first night I arrived, which is when I officially
met Jen and Abby, her 3-year-old daughter. They lived in a
small town a few miles south of where I would be spending
the next few days, so a dinner date worked perfectly.

Jen had moved back in with her parents after her divorce,
so "going back to her place" after dinner meant meeting her
folks. No pressure because having an extroverted personality,
I genuinely enjoy meeting new people. Meeting Jen was especially fortunate because she also had recently divorced and
wasn't looking for anything serious either. Knowing I was in
town for a few days meant neither of us had to make any type
of relationship happen. Instead, we could simply enjoy spending time together without feeling obligated to pursue dating
or a long-distance romance. Her parents were friendly, and
her dad loved history and quizzed me on several presidential
facts, which I truly enjoyed. From Andrew Jackson to Teddy

Roosevelt to JFK, I held my own even though I kicked myself for not knowing more answers. (Don't most of us feel that way after trivia questions?)

After Jen and I chased Abby several times around the house, we read her a story and put her to bed. We chatted more with Jen's parents before Jen and I made our way to a neighborhood pub for some pool and shuffleboard. Off the beaten path, it was the kind of place I don't imagine many tourists visit. After a few beers and laughs, we started walking back to her parents' house but stopped to overlook the dark ocean first. Only dinner had been planned ahead of time. The rest of the night was unfolding spontaneously. As a person who has always liked to plan things out, this felt like a major tidal shift for me.

Strolling along the narrow streets of her coastal town on an atypically warm spring night felt strangely comfortable. Under the light of the full moon, it struck me as odd to be walking this girl home—whom I'd only barely met—and holding hands like we were high schoolers again. It had *that* kind of feel to it. We stopped at the beach around 1 a.m. and held each other as we watched the waves roll in without the typical wind that usually accompanies all seasons on the Oregon Coast. We looked up to see a few constellations over the dark, endless ocean while chatting about our astrological signs. The ocean waves ebbed and flowed. Inhaling the fresh ocean air, I exhaled tension and grief. For the first time post-divorce I thought happiness would be possible again.

But *hope* ebbs and flows, too. Standing there with my arms wrapped around Jen made me lament not holding my ex-wife again. Missing the comforts and routines of my recently married past, I made the conscious decision to simply enjoy how things were unfolding and not overthink the present. After our meandering walk from the beach back to her home, Jen mentioned she had the next day open.

"How about we drive down the coast and visit the aquarium in Newport? It's been years since I checked it out," was the option I offered.

"Sounds fun. Let's do it!" Jen's enthusiasm injected more good vibes into our time together.

I drove back to my hotel room around 2 a.m. and did that familiar thing we all do and began replaying the "scenes" from the night in my mind before drifting off to sleep. I was beginning to see when opportunity knocks, it's ok to open an unexpected door.

The aquarium in Newport once housed the famous orca, Keiko, from the movie *Free Willy*, which was the last time I had visited the place. (For those familiar with the 1993 movie, that puts time into perspective, doesn't it?) Having been there in the late 90s with my ex-wife was another memory I felt needed to be replaced with a new experience. The memory of going there wasn't especially meaningful. But going there with Jen was another step toward crossing the bridge toward my new future without my former spouse. Perhaps she had a head start on traversing that bridge before I had a chance of doing so.

On that trip, I felt that trying to get a new sense of time and place could only happen by confronting the pain of remembering some of the old times and places from my recently married past. I was still in the early stages of the healing process and starting the new life unfolding before me. At that time, facing my fear of being alone and the pain of moving past my divorce required assigning new meanings and memories to ones I had experienced previously. Otherwise, I felt the pain that belonged in my life temporarily would remain there longer or—even worse—permanently.

Back in my hotel room, some of the arguing and issues my ex-wife and I had been having for quite a while replayed in my head. (After an enjoyable evening spent with Jen, it wasn't the way I'd hoped to fall asleep.) Bickering and being frustrated with one another happens in all relationships, but had become more persistent than either of us wanted. Our marriage was in trouble, and although it didn't include major issues like infidelity or financial problems, getting divorced was inevitable. That didn't make it any easier to process, however. In a real sense, I was being released back into the wild whether I was ready or not. Would I sink or would I swim?

After picking Jen up the next morning, we stopped for a chai latte at a local coffee joint, and it was the best chai I'd ever sipped. (Funny how the little mom-and-pop places do some things the big, franchise places can't match.) I tend to remember small details like this which some might dismiss as irrelevant. Sometimes the ordinary things in life tend to stick with me longer than I care to admit. But I've come to accept—and appreciate—that I hold onto those things not because of what they are, but because of how they make me feel. At that moment, the warm beverage was the perfect blend of sweet and spice and provided comfort to me at a time when feeling comfortable was inconsistent.

As we walked around the exhibits at the aquarium, Jen slipped her hand into mine—a simple gesture that made me feel halfway normal again because I missed things like holding hands on a regular basis. At lunch along the bay, we talked about our past relationships and some of our goals and hopes for our separate futures. Life has a funny way of presenting all of us with people who pass into and out of our lives for various reasons and during various seasons of our lives.

Not everyone we meet in life has to stay there. But everyone who comes into our life can teach us a lesson. Jen's lesson offered a new look at myself and how I could move forward. She helped me see that although I was hurting, it was a new opportunity for me to grow as a person. I've always felt there's room for continuous improvement in ourselves and our lives in general, but it was the last thing I was focused on then.

Spending time with Jen helped shed light on the idea that I would—and could—improve myself and my life in meaningful ways, which facilitated the healing process.

In the few days we spent talking and listening to each other, I learned how she was coping with her transition into singlehood. She shared her thoughts that not every relationship is meant to last forever because each of us has choices in how we grow. She helped me better understand that some relationships hold us back from reaching our fullest potential. And her kindness and willingness to do simple things like hold hands provided hope that I would find a woman—when the time was right—who would be a better fit for the person I'd eventually grow into and become.

SCOTT LOONEY 2.0

Jen said some things I needed to hear, and it restored some of my lost confidence. (Being told you're handsome, intelligent and have a great capacity for love will never dampen anyone's self-worth, right?) Confidence literally means "with trust" and Jen was providing me with the faith in myself I needed—and something marriage didn't provide.

"Divorce happens. We have to pick ourselves up and move on," I remember her saying. "Sure it hurts, but you can't wallow in it forever, and it doesn't do you any good anyway."

"I've always been a positive person, but the past six months have taken a big toll on me," I explained as I tried to put into words how unlike myself I'd been feeling since my divorce.

I told Jen how beautiful she was. And she was. I told her what a great mom she was. And by all appearances she was. And I think Jen needed to hear those things as well. After all, having trust in ourselves and others is what helps us all travel through the journey of life.

"Hey, what are your plans later tonight?" Jen asked as I dropped her off that sunny afternoon.

"I'm planning on reading a little and catching a baseball game on TV. Why?" I replied while hoping she was open to spending more time together.

"After I put Abby to bed, I was thinking we could hang out," she offered.

"Sounds good. Wanna watch a movie or something?" I was still getting used to solitude at night and adjusting to sleeping without someone next to me. So any company I had at night was always welcome.

"A movie sounds cool. Or... we could do the tarot card reading I mentioned online a few days ago. You said you'd re-consider it, remember?" she laughed.

"Or... yeah, we could do the tarot card reading," I laughed back. "See you in a while."

Since I had come to the coast to cleanse my heart and clear my head, I decided to take a detour to a beach I hadn't fully explored on any of the vacations with my ex-wife. (I soon realized there were many places ahead of me to explore.) By the time I made it to the beach, it was early evening. After a short hike, I made my way to the sand and snapped a few sunset pictures—one of my favorite pastimes whether on the beach or not. I wandered amongst the driftwood and makeshift fire pits which had undoubtedly provided warmth to partying teens and couples on countless nights over the years. The sun was starting to drop toward the clouds building up on the distant western horizon. The beautiful orange, reddish hues of a classic coastal sunset started taking shape, and I soaked it all in.

YOU'RE NEVER ALONE

At the time, I remember feeling like I was completely alone on a private beach. The beach symbolized a new chapter in life, and it felt right. Enjoying the beauty and majesty of the waves methodically arriving and receding again before crashing on top of one another always helps reset my biorhythms. I watched everything, but also watched nothing in particular. Watching campfires and waves has a similar effect on me. I can stare at both for hours and allow myself to get lost—and found—on all kinds of topics.

Standing there enjoying the peace and serenity of another gorgeous coastal sunset, a father and his two teenage daughters walked nearby. I smiled and nodded to him and the girls. I commented on the sunset, which started a conversation between me and three strangers—something I enjoy doing. After 15 to 20 minutes discussing vacations, beaches, coastal towns and such, I asked them where they were from and was surprised when they answered, "Boise."

"Seriously? That's where I live," I replied with a bit of surprise.

We discovered that I'd subbed at their friends' high school back home, and the girls told me I was known as the "cool sub." I appreciated the compliment and told them as much. Being a part-time substitute teacher and freelance writer back then, the camaraderie of other teachers and the mentoring of students was truly gratifying. Connecting with people has always been easy for me and something I genuinely enjoy doing. It has enriched my life immeasurably by providing different perspectives I may not have considered otherwise. Over the years, I've truly valued the broad perspectives my students provide. And the boost of confidence these students had indirectly given me helped trigger a career decision I would soon be making that positively impacted my travel life, too.

After wishing them a great remainder of their vacation, I made my way across the beach and back to my car with only a little light to spare. I ate a quick dinner and cleaned up my hotel room before Jen arrived.

THE DEATH CARD

Not long after welcoming Jen into my hotel room, we decided to do the tarot card reading. Shortly after contacting her online, I'd initially said no to having a reading. But when she explained it a little more, I reconsidered. Although I can't remember the exact cards she turned over that night, I do know the dreaded Death card did not come up. And I remember how easily Jen put my mind at ease by explaining that she had always interpreted the Death card to mean the death of an idea, a relationship or period in one's life and not an *actual* prediction of one's demise. I exhaled a sigh of relief. (It was good to hear it from her perspective rather than the one I'd built up in my mind.)

Jen's reading of the tarot cards involved her explaining that I was a balanced person who needed to find new ground upon which to stand. She said the questions I sought answers to regarding my divorce and the transition toward an uncertain future could be found by exploring new horizons and relying on the wisdom I had attained so far in life. (Pretty solid feedback, whether you've gone through a breakup, divorce or any other big life change.) Nothing earth-shattering was in the reading, but I appreciated her relaxed and positive outlook and the ease with which she intuitively read my psychic story. I'm glad she did a reading. At a time when some of my deductive reasoning seemed amiss, it helped me value *dis*illusionment, because it provides the opportunity to adjust our way of thinking. The reading also gave me the opportunity to try something new when new things were happening in my life nearly every day.

After she completed the reading, we spent the next few hours talking about the complexities of life—everything from our families and friends to careers and relationships. It was somewhat odd knowing that we would likely not see each other ever again after I left the coast the next morning. We talked about that too. Jen explained she wasn't the type of person who needed or expected me to stay in touch with her. Instead, she believed we were meant to spend time with each other at this particular time in both of our lives. So we accepted the idea of possibly being a romantic match but definitely not a logistical one. Besides, neither of us was seeking a relationship—especially a long-distance one—while we both were processing a major transition from years of marriage to being newly single. We'd spent some quality time together while I was visiting the coast, and it helped both of us feel a sort of normalcy we hadn't felt in a while. Meeting up the next morning for coffee was sweet, but saying goodbye was a jolt.

At the car, I hugged cute little Abby first, and she cried when Jen lifted her from my arms and placed her gently into her car seat. Unexpected tears welled up in my eyes as I watched this caring mother comfort her child. Maybe Abby's innocent heart and mind couldn't handle the transition they were in, which tugged at my emotions. My adult mind could barely fathom the realities of *my* new present at the time. Divorce had forced us all into a more fluid and unwanted state compared to the relatively comfortable and static routines of married life. The gravity of it all touched my heart, and I felt closer to them in that moment than expected.

As we pulled away after hugging, Jen pulled out a small

metal locket with the inscription: "Spread Your Wings and Fly." It was a thoughtful keepsake she knew I could use for a while during this transition period. I went to the coast for a breath of fresh air, and Jen's fresh perspective provided exactly that. And I learned that confronting our fears—whether it's the fear of being alone or dying, or both—is a necessary step in order to begin and continue the process of moving forward after a major life transition.

MOVING FORWARD

I've continued taking two to three solo trips to the coast every year because the maiden voyage proved to be one of the best decisions of my life. And each trip has been better than the previous one. Now, I have firmly planted my flag in the sand, and it no longer represents two people, but one. Looking back, if I hadn't faced my fears—and continued avoiding them instead—I may not have made myself available to the opportunities which soon came my way.

A year or so after that first trip, I went back to the restaurant where I first met Jen and Abby. I decided to write a short message on a card which I left with one of the employees to give to Jen whenever she ate there next. I wasn't seeking a reply. It was simply my way of letting her know she had helped me when I needed it most and I appreciated the time we'd spent together. Since my divorce, I've made nearly two dozen solo trips to the coast and have left three or four other notes for Jen over the years. I ask a restaurant employee each time if Jen and her daughter still eat there. As long as the answer is yes, I'll continue wishing them well by dropping off a message from time to time.

I kept the metal locket. It sits on top of my dresser so I see it every day, amidst the ebb and flow of busy work and social obligations, time with family and friends—and life in general. Whenever the rigidity of daily life begins seeping in, I start wondering—and pondering—about the journeys and chapters I've experienced since my divorce and the ones yet ahead. I had no way of knowing at the time, but my life and next chapters were just beginning to take off.

> *"You can't start the next chapter of your life*
> *if you keep re-reading the last one."*
>
> *- Anonymous*

THE TWIN CITIES AND CHICAGO:

Mental Bookmarks and Dreams

JOURNAL ENTRY (CIRCA 2014)

"I'm not sure I was ever in love with you."

I was foolish—and naive—enough to think these words were only said in soap operas and written in bad romance novels. In that context it would be funny, except my wife of 16 years actually expressed these words to me in the time between telling me she wanted a divorce and our actual divorce two months later. Of all the awful things we both were guilty of saying to each other during that awkward and painful time, these words hurt the most. To be fair, I was no saint and stated some things I regret. Obviously many things get said during hyper-emotional times, especially during a breakup or a divorce. Naturally, many things said by the people involved aren't actually what is intended, but rather an emotional outburst to the current situation. And I hope anything I said didn't stick with her as long as her aforementioned words stuck with me.

Nothing else she said even came close to hurting me as deeply as this short sentence did after spending over 18 years together as a couple. Ouch isn't nearly the right word. Dagger to the heart? Yes, but still too simplistic of a description. Cruel? Absolutely, but that's too dismissive of the impact it had on me physically, mentally and emotionally long after the divorce was final. Devastating? Yep. That's the word I found most fitting. Her words left a hole in my heart, which I realized would take a while to heal.

After getting over the initial heaviness of these words—and after moving on from our divorce—I actually felt sorry for her. I felt sorry she hadn't fully experienced the love I had shown her. I felt sorry she hadn't seemingly enjoyed all the things we said and did together for so many years. I was reminded by my family that she made her decision for her and not necessarily because of me. This didn't make sense to me initially, but makes complete sense now.

She was clearly done with that chapter of her life—which directly impacted my life—and she chose to exhibit this in the way she did at that particular time. Whatever her intentions— or *un*-intentions—were, I got over it and forgave her. Hopefully, she has forgiven me for the hurtful things I said during that awkward time between our final chapter together and the new chapters ahead of us as individuals. Eventually, I came to the conclusion that finding my future wife would be inherently more challenging because of my experiences with my ex-wife—but would be much more meaningful and rewarding as well.

And that's when I found myself in Minneapolis meeting a woman I had only met via the Words With Friends app...

I don't imagine it happens often that a non-dating app on your phone leads to meeting an incredibly kind, fun and generous person who is willing and able to make multiple travel adventures happen over the course of nearly a year. But that's exactly what happened to me in the first summer after my divorce, which was only a couple of months after my first solo trip and tarot card experience on the Oregon Coast. The timing—and the traveling opportunities that came later—were the best things that could've happened to me at that point in my life. Serendipitous? Unbelievably so.

Quite accidentally, I met Brooke on Words With Friends at a time when I was still trying to navigate the loneliest and most soul-searching period of my life. We've all been there to one degree or another. It's brutally painful at times, but necessary at times, too. Are there accidents in life, or is everything meant to happen? I'm not sure. But one thing I do know is this happy accident of meeting Brooke led to a 10-month period of unprecedented traveling adventures. I began feeling like I'd been given an opportunity to push the reset button on my life. Was my post-divorce life up to me to *choose* how I'd live it or simply the journey I was *meant* to be on? Maybe it was both.

WORDS WITH FRIENDS

My youngest brother, Monte, introduced me to Words With Friends shortly after I bought my first smartphone back in the heady days of October 2012—when my divorce was finalized—and smartphones were reaching the masses. I hadn't played the board game Scrabble in years, but felt like my vocabulary skills would serve me well on this app version of the classic game. I quickly learned how great my brother was at WWF and how awful I was. After losing the first 20 or so games to him, I remember messaging him a smart-ass quip when I finally won a game. At the time, I think my record against him sat at an impressive one win against 30 losses.

Our schedules don't allow us to play often, so we rarely

make more than one move per day—a glacial pace which some WWF players undoubtedly wouldn't have the patience for. While we live in a world that has made connecting digitally easier than ever, the disconnected feeling many of us feel overall may be due to the decreasing number of in-person interactions we experience. Since Monte and I don't see each other often, it's one way for us to stay connected, and we've been continuously playing since 2012—and I've even managed to win a few more times.

So it was one morning I woke up and drowsily opened the WWF app and—completely by accident—touched the "play someone new" button. I'm not a morning person and really wasn't interested in starting a new game with anyone. I didn't need a stranger beating me to prove what I already knew: my WWF game was weak. But that morning a complete stranger took up my accidental challenge, and we began playing a game. She beat me in record time. Surprisingly, she asked for a rematch, although I had provided little challenge.

Realizing I wasn't faring well during the second game, I messaged this WWF "bully" with a message that went something like, "Hey, take it easy on me... I'm a new player. :)"

Showing no mercy, Brooke quickly beat me in a few more games as we traded jabs via the messaging function within the app. Soon we started asking the "getting to know you" questions strangers often ask. In our back-and-forth messages, she explained she lived in Minneapolis, but grew up in Illinois. Being a lifelong baseball fan and learning she was too, I asked if she'd grown up a Chicago Cubs fan. She confirmed her Cub fandom and had been to Wrigley Field several times. I told her how jealous I was because I'd dreamed of visiting Wrigley since childhood.

TERRIFIC TIMES IN THE TWIN CITIES

We continued playing WWF into the early summer before exchanging phone numbers and then texting and calling each other throughout June and July. (Remember, this was through a non-dating app almost a year after my marriage ended.) Then a trip was planned, which included meeting in-person and going to two major league baseball games at ballparks I hadn't visited yet. I eagerly looked forward to all of it and wasn't sure what would come of the visit—if anything—between Brooke and I. At the time—which was a year after being told my marriage was over—I felt many different emotions ranging from excitement to self-doubt. Meeting a woman who could be a potential romantic match ignited curiosity, trepidation and hope.

When I flew to Minneapolis in early August, it turned out to be the first of many flights to spend time with Brooke. Peering out the window of the plane at 30,000 feet, I caught myself giggling like a kid. I smiled and reflected on the unpredictable—yet mostly positive—experiences which had arisen in less than a year after my divorce. Studies show that divorce is near the top of the most stressful events people face in life. This was certainly true for me. But it also brought me to a new, exhilarating chapter in my life, and I was becoming increasingly curious about what was ahead.

I found myself flying to a place I'd never visited to spend time with a woman I'd only recently—and accidentally—met through an online gaming app of all things. (Yes, for those of you wondering, I questioned my sanity a time or two during the flight there and back.) The official weekend itinerary included watching a Minnesota Twins game on Friday night in downtown Minneapolis and then driving to Chicago to see the Dodgers play the Cubs at Wrigley Field on Saturday afternoon. I was ecstatic to be flying to the Midwest for this adventure and especially getting to watch a game at Wrigley—something I'd dreamed about since I was a kid.

The unofficial weekend itinerary included exploring a possible romantic connection between Brooke and me. Leading up to that first weekend together, there existed a spark between us. And at times during that weekend we physically acted on that spark. Almost a year after my divorce, I'd started to forget what physical connection felt like, so naturally I was happy when we allowed the sparks to fly. However, while flying home and reflecting on that first weekend together, the realization hit that I was nowhere near emotionally ready to begin a relationship—especially a long-distance one—with Brooke or any other woman for that matter. I openly communicated that to her, and she respected the decision.

I was grateful and thankful we moved forward as friends because we had many more fun adventures ahead of us after that first weekend in the Midwest. Some of my friends wondered if Brooke may have felt like I was leading her on. Perhaps initially, but I honestly explained where I stood mentally at that time, and it was never my intent to lead her on in any way. Brooke respectfully acknowledged the decision of going forward as friends, especially since we were two adults who enjoyed each other's company and positive energy while traveling together. I felt it was the right decision not to explore a relationship then—and still do now.

After being with one woman for 18 years, it took a while post-divorce to explore the opportunities available to me as a newly single man. In a long-term relationship, you know your partner and vice versa. Not so much when you're single. And being single was still something I was getting accustomed to even a year after my divorce. After returning from meeting Jen on the Oregon Coast in March, online dating wasn't something I felt ready for. (Meeting Brooke *accidentally* through a non-dating app a couple of months later still makes me shrug in disbelief.) Being with someone new felt both exciting and awk-ward that first weekend when I flew to Minneapolis. I was ready for physical interaction with someone new, but I was definitely far from mentally ready—even though it was nearly a year post-divorce.

When landing in Minneapolis to meet Brooke in-person that first time, internal butterflies made it challenging to hold back some nervous laughter. In the early stages of transition-ing into a more go with the flow mindset, I was embarking on an adventure chock full of unknowns. Oddly, it felt comforta-ble to be a little uncomfortable. I had been encouraged by some friends and family members to go to Minnesota, while I had been discouraged by others who thought it was foolish.

Maybe it *was* foolish of me to buy a plane ticket to fly half-way across the country to meet a woman I'd only chatted with for a couple of months. But much of my life was in reset mode then and I decided that life is too short to later regret not tak-ing some chances. So that trip was a calculated risk I was will-ing to take. And I've never once regretted the decision to go. Besides, I began caring much less about people's perceptions of me after my divorce. This was when I reached a new bench-mark for not giving a damn what others thought and, psycho-logically, this was as important of a transition as any I was going through at the time.

When Brooke picked me up at the baggage claim area, the size of her smile was only outdone by the size of her heart. And I had no idea this would be the beginning of one of the most adventurous periods of my life. Had anyone told me that sum-mer I'd be embarking on a series of adventures that started with an accidental WWF game with a stranger, I would've laughed them out of the room. As we were driving to Brooke's home in a suburb of Minneapolis, the irony struck me that I'd purchased a plane ticket to meet a stranger a few months after receiving a metal locket from another stranger with the inscription "Spread Your Wings and Fly." I was literally and metaphorically doing both.

Being open and grateful for the opportunity when it presented itself, I was taking a chance my previous self would've thought foolish. And doing so was about to provide some amazing experiences which served as a catalyst to my future chapters. By the time the weekend ended, I began imagining good things coming into my life again. I also allowed myself to start dreaming of traveling to places I had slowly given up on pursuing during my marriage. (See Wrigley Field, Fenway Park, etc.) Being divorced allowed me to rediscover some passions I had for baseball and travel, which helped me move forward. Being single again and no longer having to explain why I wanted to do this or that was definitely an adjustment for me. Getting used to my new single status was extremely liberating because it offered a glimpse ahead at an independence I would come to embrace but hadn't felt for many years.

Opportunities and friendships can be fleeting. As a result, one of my post-divorce mantras became: do things *when* you can, *while* you can. Why wait until retirement to chase dreams and travel adventures? We should all take some chances and be grateful we did. Alternatively, we can safely remain in our comfort zones and be fine. But I learned on that first trip to the Midwest, specifically, that adventures often happen when you least expect *or plan for* them. I wasn't a person many would consider as being very flexible. (Anyone else out there Type A?) But I began feeling myself changing and taking on more of a growth mindset, which is essentially believing that each of us is in control of improving our abilities and situations. My journey toward transitioning into learning more about who I was as a newly single guy and where I could go in life—both literally and figuratively—was beginning to take off. (Yes, that awful pun was intended. I'm sorry. Or am I?)

Being in Minneapolis and then Chicago with Brooke over that extended weekend and fulfilling a childhood dream of watching a ballgame in Wrigley Field gave me goosebumps on several occasions. There are times in our lives when we may not remember exactly what we were thinking or doing as a moment happened, but we realize some moments are meaningful to our present and our future as they unfold. That was definitely one of those times for me, and I vividly recall mentally bookmarking as many moments as possible throughout the weekend. A new baseball season had officially started that spring. A new chapter in my life had officially begun as well.

MENTAL BOOKMARKS

We all remember specific, meaningful moments in our lives, and I try to make it a common practice—whether traveling or not—to *mentally bookmark* as many of these moments as possible. Throughout my life, these bookmarks have held a special place in my mind—and heart—especially since my divorce. I've learned the importance of being appreciative of the little "good things" as well as the big "good things" we get to experience in our life's journey.

Naturally, some moments in life are happy and some are not. And some of these labels change through the lens of the passing years. This is especially true when thinking about loved ones who have passed both prior to and since my divorce. The sadness I felt has transitioned into happier thoughts of having the opportunity to spend time with those people while they were here. This doesn't mean we forget those who are gone, but trying to be more grateful—and less sad—for the memories made with them is the approach I've learned to take. Each of us has moments and memories we can vividly recall experiencing with loved ones along the journey.

This ability makes us uniquely human—and uniquely fortunate. In a similar manner, the initial anger and sorrow I had when my marriage ended has transitioned into gratitude for the times we once enjoyed and for the amazing times I've experienced since.

Was meeting Brooke serendipitous? Absolutely. Were we a long-term romantic match? No. But we didn't need to be. When we first met, I hoped we could be a romantic match. However, it wasn't how I felt when returning home and having the time to reflect more on the situation. Besides not being ready to begin a relationship, some key boxes were unchecked on my mental list—none of which were Brooke's fault in any way. Initially, our chemistry had potential, but waned on my end with the physical distance between us. The combination of these factors made the decision of moving forward as friends and travel companions the best one. Brooke and I enjoyed many fun times together while becoming friends, which is ultimately what I'm most grateful for. Life can be tricky and challenging to navigate at times, while at other times it seems to flow smoother than expected. This was the beginning of a period in my life when times flowed better than I'd ever allowed myself to imagine.

GRATITUDE

I've met some great people and have seen some amazing cities, landscapes and sunsets throughout my travels—before and after my divorce. Several of those experiences happened because of my friendship with Brooke. Her generosity made some trips possible during a time period when I was on a tight budget due to residual bills from the divorce and some unforeseen medical bills. Additionally, I enrolled in grad school for the upcoming spring to pursue certification in education. (An over-priced decision I'm still paying for literally and figuratively.) Showing and expressing gratitude—verbally and through actions—are vitally important, and I try to make sure the people I'm around know they are appreciated. I've always believed the more gratitude you show, the more you'll appreciate the good things in life rather than dwelling on the not-so-good aspects.

Showing and expressing gratitude to people isn't difficult, and it's a very powerful way of connecting as humans. By being grateful—whether through words or actions—you're showing someone they matter to you and you're not taking their kindness for granted. Brooke opened my eyes and changed my perspective toward allowing others to do nice things for me even if it made me feel guilty psychologically at times. The bottom line is, we all deserve the best in life. I learned to allow people to help and do nice things for me, and stopped feeling guilty. Instead, I realized that feeling and expressing as much gratitude as possible and then paying it forward when you are able to is a winning combination. Your life and the lives around you will be positively impacted, which is ultimately good for everyone.

HOPES AND DREAMS

There were times over those 10 months when I would decline Brooke's generous offers for travel because I felt guilty. She would remind me that if she didn't want to spend time with me and didn't have the means, then she wouldn't be asking me to join her. She made a compelling argument. (I mean, would you say no to that?) So, although I paid my way for some trips—and declined going on a few others—I accepted several of her travel offers. And I'm glad I did. The next 10 months became an unprecedented time of travel—up to that point in my life at least—and provided some amazing experiences I'll never forget. Allowing myself to dream again helped create even more mental bookmarks going forward and started putting my divorce further behind me.

My divorce demoralized me and left me feeling broken in many ways. It obviously left me feeling despair on several levels, too. However, I came to realize how fortunate I was to have been given the opportunity of traveling with Brooke, who had been a stranger only a couple months earlier. By showing and telling her how grateful I was, it helped energize, heal and bring hope that better things were ahead. Having hopes and dreams is vital—especially during important transition periods in our lives—and everyone deserves to have them in life. Hope keeps us motivated and focused on better things in our future chapters.

I was constantly experiencing new things with people I was fortunate to meet after my divorce. And I was extremely fortunate to find hope and begin dreaming again during a difficult transition period, and it made all the difference in my life going forward. The process of moving on was not easy and I had a lot of help from friends and family. They reminded me that challenges should make, but not break us. (Again, easier said than done.) Learning from the challenges we face makes us stronger people, even if it may not feel that way at times. Gratitude and hope are extremely important, and I was beginning to fully appreciate the uplifting power of both as my growth process—and life—continued to unfold.

"Faced with demoralization, gratitude has the power to energize. Faced with brokenness, gratitude has the power to heal. Faced with despair, gratitude has the power to bring hope."

– Robert Emmons

And that's when I found myself sitting in Wrigley Field for the first time watching the Dodgers and Cubs on a perfect summer Saturday afternoon before being ushered out by a team employee...

A Bucket List item of mine is to watch a ballgame in every Major League Baseball ballpark. So naturally I was excited when my first full night in Minneapolis was spent at Target Field watching a ballgame. Brooke acquired corporate tickets to an Astros-Twins game, and we were fortunate to have VIP treatment for the game. After handing off the car keys to the valet, we walked into a restaurant located behind home plate and underneath the stadium. It was a full-service restaurant serving pasta, prime rib, seafood and also ballpark food like nachos and hot dogs. Almost anything a person wanted to eat was available. You could hear the radio broadcast of the game, and at least a dozen TV screens positioned around the restaurant meant fans could listen and watch the ballgame from anywhere. You could feasibly feast on prime rib the whole game and never miss a pitch. Not that I would do such a thing, but a person could. (And yes, it briefly crossed my mind.)

GREEN CATHEDRALS

I've been intrigued by baseball stadiums going back to my childhood. I love the historic parks still in use and some of the ballparks torn down long before I was born. No matter the time period, all MLB stadiums are unique and should be enjoyed for more than simply watching a ballgame. Each ballpark I've had the opportunity to visit and explore offers something different in terms of vantage points, scoreboards, food, fans and history. Since every ballpark is different, I'm intentional about appreciating the time I have at each one. Staying in the moment as experiences happen in our lives is integral to appreciating them fully. Like our different journeys in life, each of us has our own unique experiences along the way. If we only focus on the game, we miss out on the other elements that make the experience—including the game—more special. (I remind myself of this handy life metaphor often because it's easy to forget at times that the *journey* is every bit as important as the *destination*.)

Another element I love about ballparks is that the collective history of our uniquely American sport of baseball is woven into the fabric of each of these green cathedrals—just as it is woven into the history of our country. Baseball games are experienced by thousands (and sometimes millions) of people—whether it's online, TV, radio, or in-person—and become shared experiences which provide memories that bind fans to one another. These experiences link fans of other generations to each other as well. In this sense, we become part of the community in which the ballparks reside but also the larger community of fans at the national and international levels. Baseball also has a certain mythology woven into it—the players, the uniforms, the ballparks, the teams, the eras—and the special connection to the past, the present, and the future is palpable when I visit these majestic houses of baseball worship.

After enjoying the delicious pre-game meal, Brooke and I made the short walk to our seats, which were about 10 rows up from home plate and near the Minnesota Twins dugout on the first base side. I remember laughing like a kid in a candy store when realizing I could fill containers full of M&Ms, Milk Duds, and other sweets and refill them at any point during the game. (Go ahead and laugh, but I'm still a kid at heart.) Brooke giggled as I filled up a container (or three) of M&Ms to snack on during the game. Again, we should remember to be grateful for the little "good things" as well as the big "good things" life offers us along the way.

"We get VIP treatment for tonight's game and you are most excited about the refillable candy containers?" she laughed.

"Do you *see* all the different candies they have?!" I replied excitedly, as if she had somehow missed them.

Of course, I completely appreciated the VIP treatment, and it made me giddier than I was letting on. (But the all-inclusive candy? Well done, Minneapolis, well done!) It was a beautiful summer night for baseball, and two of Brooke's friends joined us for the game. The four of us laughed and talked baseball while enjoying some of the excellent local beers. Our seats were cushioned and felt like mini, weatherproof recliners. Everything was part of the VIP package. Not a bad way to begin a weekend of fulfilling a few childhood dreams.

On that Friday night in early August, the Minnesota Twins were treating fans to a fireworks show after the game. During the pre-game dinner, Brooke and I talked about needing to get a reasonable start on Saturday morning for our road trip to Chicago. Staying for the fireworks show after Friday night's game—which we both wanted to see—would still give us a decent amount of sleep before our drive the next day. What we didn't expect was the Astros-Twins game lasting 13 innings. We knew we had to get up early for the six-hour drive to Chicago the next morning since the first pitch at Wrigley Field was set for 3 p.m. on Saturday.

In the spirit of the long weekend, Brooke and I decided to enjoy it all—including the post-game fireworks—because who knew when we'd be able to do it again. And I'm glad we did because, despite making many trips to Minneapolis after that first weekend, I haven't been back to Target Field. (Again, we should all do things when we can, while we can.)

When the game finally ended with a win by the Twins on Friday night—actually early Saturday morning—we headed straight to valet parking, which fortunately allowed us to escape downtown traffic quickly. We made it to Brooke's house for about five hours of sleep before waking and starting our trip to Chicago. Shortly before waking up that morning, I vividly remember dreaming about a conversation I'd had with my ex-wife the previous summer.

"I'd love to go to Wrigley Field for a game this summer," mentioning it as I had regularly for several years.

"Yeah, I know. Maybe next summer," was her reply in what had become an annual conversation during our marriage.

Our commitments to our jobs, families and friends kept us from ever committing to a trip to Chicago. So with every passing summer I gave up a little bit more on the dream of getting to watch a Cubs game at Wrigley Field. Waking up that morning made me appreciate the trip and the day ahead even more.

Despite not getting as much sleep as planned, I looked forward to the road trip and the game—especially since it would be my first time at Wrigley Field. Sometimes opportunities don't go as planned, but that's ok. I was learning to go with the flow more at that time. And although I was a little concerned about being tired for the road trip and game, it was easy to rise to the occasion knowing I'd be at Wrigley Field that afternoon. (And it's always easier to rally when on vacation, right?)

A PERFECT DAY

We left Minneapolis that morning with caffeinated Starbucks beverages in hand for our road trip to The Windy City. Along the way, we talked about Friday night's extra inning game, how much we both loved road trips—and the requisite snacks—and about life in general. We took turns driving on our way to Illinois. Brooke and I liked a lot of the same music, shared a passion for baseball, and we always had lots to talk about, so our road trips were fun. She would quiz me on base-ball history and history in general, which I loved. (Did I mention I'm a baseball history nerd?) While I was driving—and couldn't simply look up the answers—she asked me to name as many World Series Champs chronologically from 1903 to the present as possible. I loved the challenge. That's over a century of World Series champions, so I didn't get anywhere close to all of them right. But I remember Brooke being impressed with my knowledge of the early years of the 20th century, which has always been a period in baseball history I love learning about.

Because of my appreciation of ballparks and being an extrovert, I try to soak in the local culture perhaps a little more than the average visiting fan. I love talking to fellow baseball fans in their ballparks. It's fun to meet new people this way and learn about their team, stadium and city. And no other sport in America has teams playing games in venues that opened in 1912 (Boston's Fenway Park) or 1914 (Chicago's Wrigley Field). While a stadium doesn't have to be old to have an interesting history, the grand old ballparks are truly *gems* in our country. Again, getting to the stadium for the game is the goal of every fan, but appreciating the journey to and from—and around—the ballpark is key to fully enjoying the experience. (I'm positive there's a metaphor for life in there somewhere.)

CHICAGO IS... MY KIND OF TOWN

If you've been to Wrigley Field, you'll completely understand this part of the story. If you haven't been to Wrigley Field for a Cubs game, I hope you do so at least once in your life. Even non-baseball fans have told me that watching a baseball game at Wrigley Field is special. Growing up in Idaho in the 1980s and 90s, my family constantly had WGN on in the background—which broadcast most Chicago Cubs games—during the baseball season. During those years—with the exception of 1984, 1989 and 2003—the Cubbies weren't considered a great team for many baseball seasons. However, Wrigley Field was always considered a gem regardless of how bad the Cubs were playing. The Cubs generally played the role of underdog, which made it easier to root for them. (It's almost un-American *not* to root for the underdog, isn't it?) And watching and listening to Harry Caray—the voice of the Cubs during my childhood—made it impossible not to hope and cheer for the Cubs to win a World Championship for the city of Chicago and Cubs fans everywhere.

As a kid watching games on TV, I always loved the green, ivy-covered brick walls and the fact Wrigley Field was built right into a neighborhood back in 1914. It fascinated me the same way Fenway Park did when I was growing up; the difference being that we didn't have an opportunity to watch many Red Sox games out west, except for the occasional Sunday night game on ESPN and on the NBC Saturday Game of the Week when I was a youngster. So Wrigley Field and Fenway Park became two mythical places I've wanted to visit for literally decades.

Both of these green cathedrals have asymmetrical fields which creates all kinds of opportunities for odd hops, bounces and triples. The sight lines and various angles can be quirky, but many baseball fans see it as part of the charm these historic and beautiful ballparks offer. As a kid, I could *feel* the charm and history of Wrigley Field coming through the TV screen. My siblings and I watched the Bleacher Bums singing "Take Me Out to the Ballgame" every 7th inning stretch—led by long-time announcer Harry Caray—during all of those endless summer ballgames of my youth. For as far back as I can remember, I wanted to be taken out to the ballgame to be part of the crowds in Fenway Park and Wrigley Field.

So getting to spend my first game at Wrigley Field on a beautiful summer Saturday was very special because it was a place I'd fallen in love with years before. Adding to the special day, Brooke scored us amazing seats not far behind the Dodger dugout on the first base side. And the trip fortunately fell on a weekend when I was able to find a flight that fit my schedule— and budget—and my Dodgers happened to be playing the Cubs. (Ever have those days that feel like you have a permanent smile?) At a point in my life when I was starting over, it felt appropriate to be experiencing some childhood dreams along the way.

FROM BROOKLYN TO L.A. TO BOISE?

I became a Los Angeles Dodger fan as a teen because the team was often on TV during the 80s and 90s. I pursued learning the history of the franchise from its beginnings in Brooklyn in the 1880s up through when Jackie Robinson became the first Black player to break the color barrier in major league baseball in 1947. The history of the franchise and his story appealed to me then—and means even more now—because I've always believed in and supported equality and human rights issues.

As children, our parents instilled in each of us six kids the right way to treat people. We were taught to treat everyone with respect and equality—no matter what gender, race or religion the person happened to be—and all of us are better off for it. I'm fortunate to have many friends from diverse cultural, racial and religious backgrounds, and my life has been richer because of this. Having exposure to all of the perspectives which diversity offers has provided a wealth of knowledge I otherwise wouldn't have been fortunate to experience. If you only seek one perspective, that's all you'll know. I've always chosen to seek other perspectives rather than solely my own. Applying this concept to baseball has led me to being a diehard Dodger fan with a big soft spot for the Chicago Cubs. (Some people understand this completely, while others do not, which is fine by me.)

THE FRIENDLY CONFINES OF WRIGLEY FIELD

From the moment we walked through the gates and I glimpsed the beautiful green field—and the dark green, ivy-covered outfield brick wall—I had goosebumps, and my eyes started filling with happy tears. (I was standing in Wrigley freakin' Field!) The tears, mental reality pinches and smiles weren't only coming from my lifelong love for baseball; they were also based on the realization that my ex-wife and I had talked about going to Wrigley in the summer of 2013, but our marriage ended in October 2012—much like the Dodger season had that same month—unceremoniously. So I assumed there was no chance of going to Wrigley Field the next summer after our divorce. And yet, under entirely unpredictable circumstances—and with a person unknown to me the previous summer—I made it to Chicago anyway. At times, life can be a trip, both literally and figuratively, if you allow it to be.

The Dodgers won the game—which was icing on the cake to a perfect day—but a loss wouldn't have dampened any part of that day. Quite simply, and in the most hopelessly romantic baseball fan way possible, it was one of the best days of my life. It felt like I'd somehow redeemed myself by making it to Wrigley Field that summer—despite unexpectedly divorcing the year before—and also making good on a boyhood dream.

I was grateful for so many things that day. The road trip from Minneapolis, the perfect weather, the amazing seats

Brooke pulled off, the traditional Chicago Dog and Old Style beer—both must-haves at Wrigley Field—singing "Take Me Out to the Ballgame" with the Wrigley faithful during the 7th inning stretch, and walking around the ballpark taking pictures from every angle after the final out. Brooke left the ballpark after the game ended to get the car. I had pictures to take and wanted to see the ballpark from additional vantage points.

I explained my MLB Ballpark Bucket List entailed walking around and taking pictures from various perspectives on my first visit to each ballpark. Since it was Wrigley Field, I spent more time walking around than I had at some of the other ballparks on my list. Besides, I wasn't ready to leave simply because the game was over. (Some readers might make the connection that life isn't over just because breakups and divorces happen. And I couldn't agree with you more.) I could've stayed forever, but a friendly Cubs employee escorted me out of the ballpark. Brooke was patiently waiting, and she giggled when I explained how he'd personally walked me to the exit. I took my time and relished every moment that day since being there was the realization of a boyhood dream, and I didn't know when I'd be back.

SPREADING MY WINGS

Like a ballplayer stuck on one team for too many years and being released suddenly, I was now a free agent in life. (My friend Manny and I often say everything goes back to baseball, and this is yet another example.) I was choosing to spread my wings and fly instead of staying in my comfort zone. And I'm extremely happy I did. Expressing my gratitude to Brooke over the course of that amazing weekend allowed me to move psychologically from feelings of guilt to gratitude. Keep an open mind to people, places and events because you never know when your next opportunity for adventure will happen. By dreaming and visualizing good times ahead, it helped me get over my divorce slowly but surely. Being grateful allowed me to appreciate the journey I was on and not just the various destinations I was visiting. And one more childhood dream was still in store for me that weekend before I flew home. My new journey continued to surprise me as unexpected doors to future chapters began opening.

> *"Heartbreak and hope are not mutually exclusive.*
> *We can be angry and sad and filled with longing for*
> *something we cannot have, and simultaneously we can*
> *be grateful for what we've got—aware, for reasons we'd*
> *never choose, of what really matters and what doesn't."*
>
> *- Lennon Flowers*

Update: Brooke and I were friends for a season of our lives and lost touch for a while as distance and life tend to have that effect, but I always felt our paths would cross again. We spent time catching up in the summer of 2016 before drifting apart again. During the Covid-19 pandemic in 2020, she reached out and started a game with me on Words With Friends. Our games have been evenly matched—mostly.

IOWA:

The Field of Dreams

AUTHOR'S NOTE

The movie *Field of Dreams* opened in theaters in 1989 and starred Kevin Costner and James Earl Jones, among others. Baseball fans generally agree it is a timeless, classic film. Scenes in the movie have left many grown men crying, especially when the lead character, Ray Kinsella, has a chance to play catch with his father (who passed away years earlier). I watch *Field of Dreams* every year, and that particular scene chokes me up every time—especially in the years since my father passed away in 2008. One of the many themes explored in the movie is the transition males pass through when entering their mid-life years. For many, it's a difficult transition and a time of questioning careers, relationships and becoming—or perhaps avoiding becoming—like their fathers.

The movie is adapted from the book *Shoeless Joe* written by W.P. Kinsella and it's one of the main reasons I became interested in baseball history. I was curious to learn about the players who had played in the majors long before I was born. As a result of reading the book and watching the movie, my unquenchable love of baseball history was ignited. When I was younger, I added Shoeless Joe Jackson to my list of all-time favorite baseball players. The movie is mainly set in Iowa, which is why many baseball fans have made a trek there during their lives—a pilgrimage of sorts. I was fortunate to make my pilgrimage to Iowa the first summer after my divorce.

And that's when I found myself playing baseball with a group of strangers surrounded by cornfields in Iowa...

After leaving Wrigley Field on Saturday, Brooke and I went to one of Chicago's legendary pizzerias, Lou Malnatti's. My first experience with deep dish, Chicago-style pizza did not disappoint. (It's probably a good thing I don't live in Chicago; my waistline would continuously expand.) We then checked into a swanky downtown hotel and walked a few blocks for a nightcap. It was the quintessential Chicago experience, and we fit it all into one day. It was a wonderful way to wrap up one of the best days of my life. And that's saying a lot because I've had so many phenomenal days in my life. Reflecting on these times allows me to appreciate them even more as time goes by.

I was hyperaware of it being the kind of day I may only experience a handful of times in my life. Living in the moment, I clearly remember soaking up everything I possibly could. In the past, I've been guilty of focusing on the next big vacation or milestone celebration instead of opening my mind to the endless possibilities of life that happen between the big, planned events. This is why I constantly remind myself to appreciate moments as they happen and not focus on the *planned* experiences we all celebrate like birthdays and vacations.

Brooke and I had gone to baseball games in Minneapolis and Chicago over the weekend, but the journey included so much more than getting to watch games at two ballparks. I was in the beginning of a transition in my life at a time when many men experience a midlife crisis. And I was continuing to process my divorce as well. (Not a great two-for-the-price-of-one deal.) In many ways, I was hitting the reset button on my life while also dealing with approaching middle age. A side trip to Iowa may not have rescued me from either situation, but it definitely helped me move forward in the process.

On Sunday, Brooke and I spent time with her family, and I enjoyed meeting everyone. In true Midwest fashion, they were a welcoming family, and we ate some delicious food and laughed together before Brooke and I left the next morning to begin the drive back to Minneapolis.

Being around her family reminded me of the closeness and warmth of my own family. It also reminded me of not having in-laws anymore. My in-laws treated me like family from the beginning, and I always appreciated them for doing so. (And I still keep in touch with some in-laws from my married life.) That morning, as we left Illinois and drove into Iowa, I ran the idea by Brooke of stopping outside the small town of Dyersville and visiting the site where much of the movie *Field of Dreams* was filmed. I felt kind of like a kid sitting in the backseat asking mom if we could go get ice cream.

"You know, we'll be driving close to where *Field of Dreams* was filmed a long time ago. It would be really cool to check it out," I mentioned without trying to sound too much like an excited child.

"Giddyup," Brooke replied with a smile. The term meant 'cool' and was one of her favorite sayings. And obviously, I was giddy about the giddyup!

On that trip, meeting Brooke in person and going to Wrigley Field were the primary reasons I flew to the Midwest. But being open to an unplanned experience in Iowa—of all places—provided another amazing life moment I'll never forget. Having the freedom to venture 50 miles out of the way—

maybe 100 miles is more accurate—allowed me to stop limiting myself to solely predetermined plans. Limiting what you're capable of experiencing in life will only put limits on how you'll write your next chapters. (Who wants to limit themselves in this *one* life we get to live?) In my married life, I would've been content simply flying to Chicago for a game at Wrigley Field and then flying home. As a result of my post-divorce experiences, I realized it was better to "spread my wings and fly" and take an unplanned detour to the Field of Dreams in Iowa because the opportunity presented itself.

When married, we kept a schedule that some considered rigid because we typically planned many social events with friends and family weeks or months in advance. Some people would give us a hard time for keeping such a busy calendar. We rarely deviated from the plans we'd set. This reliability was comforting in some ways but also made me realize the creature of habit I'd become. Married life wasn't necessarily boring because I appreciated the predictability it provided. But the complete upheaval of my routines which divorce forced me to adapt to was stressful at first. With all the adventures during the first year of being re-singled, I began to see unpredictability and spontaneity as positives instead of negatives.

On this trip, there was an awareness that the sky was the limit for my future unwritten chapters. For some, this mindset has been second nature since they were young. But for me, this mindset was something I was finally allowing myself to embrace. This set my brain in motion to grow and evolve in ways I hadn't thought of before. I realized how constrained I'd been in my marriage regarding following my passions. We'd taken trips to some baseball games while married—we even had some fun doing so. However, it was only after divorce when I realized how limited I'd felt by the literal and figurative bonds of my marriage.

After feeling disconnected from some of my passions—especially traveling to new places and seeing different ballparks around the country—these unplanned post-divorce adventures reignited the possibilities of doing things and going places I'd started giving up on. I enjoyed most of the trips we'd taken throughout all those years of marriage, but I started feeling like some of the places I'd wanted to visit since childhood were going to have to wait even longer. At the time, I told myself this was all part of the give and take of being married and resolved to accept that's how life goes. But being divorced made me understand life doesn't have to be that way. Starting with the adventures with Brooke, I realized my future could allow for traveling anywhere—with the proper saving up of funds, of course. Looking back, my travels have provided many valuable perspectives which helped me move past my divorce. While healing and understanding my life was starting anew, I had a positive energy I hadn't felt in years.

"IF YOU BUILD IT, THEY WILL COME"

Some people I've told this story to—non-baseball fans in particular—laugh at the notion of wanting to spend time in the middle of Iowa on a baseball field that was part of a 1989 Kevin Costner movie set. But if you're a fan, you know *Field of Dreams* is not your average baseball movie. My mom and siblings have all watched it multiple times, and we still quote lines from the movie from time to time. (My older brother Bob does a spot-on impression of James Earl Jones giving his baseball history speech.) When telling my baseball friends and family about this part of the weekend journey, some were actually more interested in hearing about my afternoon in Iowa than my story about going to Wrigley Field in Chicago for the first time. Both were very special and meaningful experiences, but for different reasons.

So 48 hours after having one of the best experiences of my life in Chicago, I found myself playing baseball outside Dyersville for a couple hours with complete strangers. The sun was set high against a backdrop of a thin layer of clouds, which provided for a hazy and mildly humid summer day. From the moment we turned onto the road leading to the old farmhouse and baseball field, there was something magical about being there. (Of course, loving *Field of Dreams* combined with my baseball history nerdiness naturally enhanced my feelings of excitement.) As we parked, I quickly grabbed my baseball mitt—which I had taken into Wrigley Field with hopes of catching a ball—and walked up to the field where four other guys were already playing catch. I had butterflies in my stomach as I stood there at the edge of the dirt before stepping onto the hallowed grass like Kevin Costner's character, Ray Kinsella, had done in the movie all those years before.

"You guys mind if I join you?" was how I began my transition back to being 12 years old—for a couple of hours anyway.

"Of course not!" one of the guys in a Minnesota Twins cap replied, waving me onto the field.

"We're about to start hitting, so grab a spot anywhere you want," his buddy added.

I found out later these two friends were passing through and also dreamed of someday playing on this field located amongst the tall, green cornfields outside Dyersville. Well, that day was our *someday*. We were five baseball fans who didn't need to know each other to enjoy the simple happiness of throwing and catching a baseball with one another. Fortunately, one of the guys brought his wooden bat, so he was first to take his turn hitting—a nod to one of the many unwritten rules of baseball.

CONNECTING WITH THE PAST, PRESENT AND FUTURE OF THE GAME OF BASEBALL

If you haven't hit a baseball with a wooden bat, there is something special about swinging and making contact with a hardball. The sound and feel is better than hitting with an aluminum or composite bat. Most high school and college players play with composite bats while all major leaguers use wooden bats. When ball meets bat, the resulting 'crack' sound a wooden bat makes is unmistakable. Most fans can tell whether a ball has been weakly hit or has been crushed solely by the sound it makes.

No matter the type of bat, there's a shared experience when hitting a baseball because you share the physical ability with all the people who played before you—those who play today, and those who will play tomorrow. It's the same with attending a major league game. You are in the crowd with thousands of other fans who are cheering on the home team—along with some who aren't. You're sharing an experience with others who have cheered at that ballpark long before you, the ones at the game with you that day, and the fans who will be cheering at future games long after you're gone.

Catching a home run or foul ball has eluded me in all of the major league games I've attended—so far, at least. But having so many wonderful memories, which I've taken home with me, means snagging a ball would simply be icing on the cake. Everyone leaves the ballpark with a shared experience but also individual memories which many recall years later because *something* at that game was significant to them. Whether it's the players and teams we are there to watch, spectacular plays made during the game, or special moments shared with friends and family, most fans have something meaningful to take home—either in their hands or in their hearts.

Although there were many reasons to be excited that afternoon, I was a little nervous about the chance of hitting with a wooden bat. It was the first time I'd hit and thrown a baseball in several years. So it was a fitting way for my symbolic re-entry into childhood to continue. In a very real sense, I was starting over in life, and the experience of living out a childhood dream felt appropriate then. We don't often get a second chance to live our lives differently after a dramatic shift takes place. So feeling like a kid again at a time when I was literally resetting my life was extraordinarily meaningful. I felt like Shoeless Joe Jackson in the movie who was given a second chance to play baseball after being banned for life while he was alive. (I even researched and wrote a couple of college papers about this topic but won't bore you with the details here.) Throughout that weekend spent in the Midwest, I realized the need to make the most of this unexpected second chance. I now had the opportunity—and freedom—to write the next chapters in my life. This was a great way to begin the process.

As a kid, I was a pitcher who lacked a great fastball but could throw a better-than-average curveball. I was known for having great control, and I used the curveball effectively, but not effectively enough to play past high school. When not pitching, I played center field like my older brother Bob. We both loved playing center field, but he was much better at it than I'd been. (I hang my hat on being the most consistent pitcher in the family while he made plays in the outfield much more consistently than I ever did.) In Iowa, it felt natural to jog to the outfield like I had for all those practices and games in the summers of my childhood. Throwing and catching the ball while basking in the experience felt like the endless summer days of my youth. Was this field the fountain of youth for baseball players and fans like in the movie? That afternoon, I was starting to feel like it might be.

As the five of us shagged fly balls and fielded grounders,

we gave each other a hard time, but also complimented each other when someone had a solid hit or made a nice catch. (I'm only partially joking about turning back the hands of time and feeling 12 years old again.) That day it felt like home on a beautifully manicured piece of land carved out of cornfields that seemingly went to the horizon. Roaming the outfield in the middle of Iowa felt exactly like when I roamed center field on the ballfield near my childhood home. That park was a special place my family and I had watched and played baseball in for so many summers—all those summers ago.

When it was my turn to hit, a guy traveling from Los Angeles with his girlfriend to visit family in Ohio handed me the bat. He wore a Cincinnati Reds cap and asked me about my Dodger cap—which I wear often—and where I was from. During a brief water break, it was fun telling him about being an Idaho boy who grew up watching the Cubs and how I'd fallen in love with the history of the Brooklyn and Los Angeles Dodgers as a teen. He paused briefly and produced a ball out of his pocket and handed it to me.

"Well, this ball needs to go to you then," he said with a smile and handed me a worn, autographed baseball with multiple signatures.

"Wow... thanks, man!" I replied as the feeling of being a kid again surged through me. "Who signed this ball?" I asked like the 12-year-old me would have.

"A bunch of old Dodgers... Steve Garvey, Ron Cey..." he began listing off some great Dodger players from the years before I officially became a fan. "Sorry, but we needed a ball earlier and played catch with it before you got here, so some of the names might be a little smudged."

Looking down at the roughed-up ball, I laughed and said, "No worries, man. It's still a cool ball."

The other guys were standing around and one shouted from the outfield, "You gonna hit or we gonna chat all day?"

We chuckled as I walked toward home plate for my turn at bat. Since I hadn't swung a wooden bat and hit a hardball for years, it felt so good to make contact again. None of us were there to compete or see how many people we could strike out. Instead, we were there to play on a baseball field we'd only seen in the movie. We laughed and joked like we were childhood teammates. At the end of hitting a bunch of balls—and missing some as well—I switched sides of the plate and batted left-handed. A few of the guys yelled out, "Show off!" which was another line from the movie and made me laugh. I was fully in the moment and enjoying everything about the experience. (Who knew if or when I'd be able to do this again?)

As right-handers, my younger brother Dave and I taught ourselves how to bat left-handed when we were teens. During the summers after our city league seasons ended, we would play baseball games and practice together in the outfield of our local ballpark only a block away from our house. Dave and I set up a mini-league every summer to play against each other and we had fun picking MLB teams and batting like the players on those teams. We tried to mimic the batting stances of all those players from our youth, and both of us became quite skilled at batting like some of the big leaguers.

When Dave batted like Don Mattingly, who was a lefty, I would often try to sneak a curveball by him and nearly every damn time he would crush it! So whenever he mimicked Mattingly's batting stance, I started throwing fastballs on the corners of the plate, but absolutely no curves. It got to the point where we both liked hitting lefty more than righty. Ken Griffey, Jr. was a favorite player of all of ours and trying to hit like him made me appreciate his beautiful swing all the more. In a couple of our Babe Ruth League summer games, Dave and I both batted lefty and got some hits that counted. Our coach wasn't convinced we should keep batting lefty, but our teammates cheered, and we were happy to prove we could do it during an actual game. Switching sides at the plate was sort of a reversal befitting that day for me—we were men playing like kids and no longer kids trying to mimic the play of men. And some of the aches and pains my adult self felt the next day weren't quite as painful when I thought about the memories made that afternoon.

While I was hitting, I glanced over at Brooke as she sat attentively on the small wooden bleacher along the first base side of the field, which is exactly where it was positioned in the movie. We both smiled as she could see the joy the experience was bringing to me and the other guys. Batting left-handed, I connected on my best hit of the day to end my turn at home plate. As it made a nice, high arc deep into right field before dropping into the freshly mowed grass—approaching the corn—I wondered to myself how far the ball would go. It was a memorable shot to end my turn. The guys congratulated me on the wallop that landed short of the gently swaying corn-fields doubling as the outfield fence. I tipped my cap and smiled at them. Connecting with the ball—and those guys—on that day was cathartic.

Then my adult brain kicked in. I assumed Brooke might be getting tired of watching five guys hitting and throwing base-balls on this mildly humid summer afternoon. So, after hand-ing the bat to the next guy up, I grabbed my baseball glove and walked over to her.

"We can go whenever you're ready," I said, still beaming from my turn at the plate.

"And miss seeing what you were like as a boy? I've been watching you play, run and laugh like a kid, and it's amazing."

I trotted back to the outfield with the words I wanted to say to her still stuck in my throat and happy tears welling up in my eyes. I was still grinning from ear to ear as I realized the experience didn't have to end yet. If you appreciate the small moments and allow them to be meaningful as they happen, your mental scrapbook will become richer and fuller than you can possibly imagine. Standing in the outfield on a gem of a ballfield in the middle of nowhere in Iowa—a state I was passing through for the first time—made me pause and reflect how lucky I felt to be there at that particular time in my life. Getting an opportunity to sort out some psychological baggage—as I was passing through the stages of childhood and transitioning back to being a single man—was a mental state I felt fortunate to be passing through a second time.

"EASE HIS PAIN"

We played a little more but knew our time feeling like boys playing a game again was nearly up. Shoeless Joe Jackson and the rest of the ballplayers in the film knew if they "crossed the line" by leaving the ballfield it would end their time playing baseball forever. A year after my divorce, I was realizing that I needed to cross the line mentally and let go of the pain and anger of my married past. Throughout the process, I was discovering the need to face the reality that some doors permanently close in our lives and accepting that fact is vital to moving forward.

At the time, learning I was far from ready to get into a serious relationship was also important. Had I allowed myself to fall for anyone so soon after divorce, I'd be writing a completely different narrative. Growth requires learning from our experiences before being ready to move forward. The valuable lessons on that trip helped me begin doing exactly that.

Before leaving the field, we all paused for a moment on the pitcher's mound as Brooke snapped a picture. I still have that picture somewhere, and maybe it belongs next to the metal pendant I have on my dresser. That image captured five happy men feeling like boys again. We connected through a sport and a special location on a baseball diamond cut out of Iowa farmland. Although we could've added each other on social media, none of us did. The moment had been more than enough for each of us. So we waved to one another as we crossed the line, leaving the field to return to our adult lives.

As we walked off the field, one of the guys made a reference to the movie by asking, "Is this Heaven?"

"No. It's Iowa," I smiled while quoting another famous reply from the movie.

"GO THE DISTANCE"

On the drive back to Minneapolis that night, as Brooke was sleeping in the passenger seat, I reflected on the day and began wondering how far I'd be able to go in the next chapters of my life. Flying home the following day, I thought about the opportunities and newfound freedom to write new chapters in my life going forward. Instead of feeling sad about my previous life as a married man, I began to consider the new chapters I'd get to live and grow from. It was still early in the transition phase from Married Man to Single Guy. I was grateful for the amazing, fun-filled weekend in Minneapolis and Chicago. But also grateful for the time spent far from the crowds of the Twin Cities and the Windy City—in the middle of nowhere amongst the continually growing cornfields of Iowa. Grateful to have stepped back to childhood—to experience several wonderful moments—if only for a moment.

> *"We just don't recognize life's most significant moments while they're happening."*
>
> *- Archie "Moonlight" Graham*
> *(in* Field of Dreams*)*

NORTHWEST TO MIDWEST TO SOCAL:

7 MLB Games, 6 Cities, 5 States in 2 Months

JOURNAL ENTRY (CIRCA 2015): "HOPE"

Following my divorce, I had a lot of help from supportive family and friends. And hopefully I've been able to thank each of them—especially my mom and siblings—for their understanding, support and encouragement throughout the post-divorce transition period. Being surrounded by people who love me made the process of healing the deeply painful wound of a broken heart a bit easier to endure. They reminded me things would indeed get better, which provided the key ingredient—hope—in successfully transcending what I was going through. In fact, much of the time it carried me forward when my world had seemingly collapsed around me. The beautiful thing about having hope is it eventually blossoms. Many people planted the seed which helped me step out of the past, find happiness and, most importantly, see more hope in the future.

By staying as positive as possible during that time of transition, I noticed things starting to improve. As different people and experiences came into my life, it provided me with even more hope. None of this happened overnight, of course. But eventually things did get better. Now I can look back with a smile—and a few tears—at how many wonderful people I've met and experiences I've had in the past couple of years since the divorce. Obviously, had I still been married, I wouldn't have been able to enjoy these same people and experiences. Being single allowed me to build on the hope you can only see when you are able to rise above your situation and really take in the big picture more clearly. Traveling—and writing—provided the means of transcending my current situation.

And that's when I found myself cruising at night around San Diego for the first time and learning I'd be golfing the next morning with a guy I'd never met at a course I'd never played...

EPIC BASEBALL ADVENTURES

Brooke and I experienced a remarkable amount of baseball travels in the late summer of that first year following my divorce and dubbed it our Epic Baseball Adventures. Although the word epic is often overused, it was appropriate for the unprecedented amount of travel we undertook at the end of that baseball season.

Attending seven MLB games in six cities—across five states from the Northwest to the Midwest to Southern California—in August and September was incredible. At that point in my life, it was easily the most travel I'd undertaken in that amount of time. (It would later be eclipsed by some extraordinary travel I was fortunate to experience in the summer of 2019.) The trips we took in that brief span, specifically, inspired me for the travel I would later experience. Entering that first summer nearly a year following my divorce, I didn't realistically envision myself traveling anywhere with anyone. I was still figuring out a lot of things and traveling was definitely on the backburner—or so I thought.

A couple of weeks after traveling to the Twin Cities, Chicago and Iowa in early August, Brooke flew out to visit me in Idaho. I wanted to show her some of the great things my hometown had to offer. I also promised her a road trip to Seattle so she could see some of the great places we have in the Pacific Northwest. After an Angels-Mariners game at beautiful Safeco Field (later renamed T-Mobile Park) and some fun sightseeing in the Emerald City over the weekend, a plan was hatched for me to fly back to the Midwest for another baseball road trip the next weekend.

That adventure over Labor Day Weekend took us from Minneapolis through Milwaukee (for an Angels-Brewers game) and then my second trip to Wrigley Field in less than a month (for a Phillies-Cubs game). I had no idea I'd be back at Wrigley within a month of my first time there! All of this was a whirlwind of fun times. Thinking back on all of the flights, road trips and games we experienced in such a short time frame always brings a big smile to my face. *Epic* truly is the appropriate descriptor, and I was happily learning how to travel spontaneously. I was also learning to find happiness— and hope—in the past, the present, and potentially the future. Brooke was the main catalyst for this new hope. At times, we all need other people to help us see that hope exists despite the difficult times we all go through. If my post-divorce happiness—and blossoming hope—had a gardener, it was Brooke. No longer was I anchored to the sadness of the recent past because I was simultaneously enjoying the present while being inspired by a new hope for my future.

"Can you get away to San Diego?" Brooke texted one night a week after our Labor Day getaway in the Midwest.

"That sounds like fun! When ya thinking?" I texted back,

assuming it would be in October or later that fall.

"Next weekend!" She replied. "Got a conference in S.D. Be fun if you join me. Maybe catch a Padres game? Btw, your Dodgers are playing in L.A. too." It was an offer I couldn't refuse.

"You had me at baseball," I texted while laughing at how she casually mentioned the part about my Dodgers playing at home. She knew that would seal the deal for me. And it did.

This interaction was pretty typical of our friendship that started that spring while playing Words With Friends. Our accidental friendship opened the door to so many memorable experiences. The details of some of the travels in this chapter illustrate the power of positive thinking and having hope for a better tomorrow. Even when healing from a major life transition, hope and positivity can bring amazing people and experiences into your life if you keep an open mind.

So when Brooke offered the chance to meet up in southern California in late September, I jumped at it and quickly booked my flights. After all, I couldn't say no to wrapping up the baseball season with my first game in San Diego (between the Diamondbacks-Padres) and my first game at Dodger Stadium (for a Rockies-Dodgers matchup). I didn't mind going into some credit card debt if it included traveling—especially when it involved making another childhood dream come true by getting to watch my Dodgers in Los Angeles for the first time.

Upon landing in San Diego, Brooke picked me up in a convertible Mustang. As we zipped around downtown that beautiful fall night, she revealed I had a tee time the next morning at the resort course where her conference was being held. Although I was really excited about the opportunity, my pragmatic side worried about not having packed my golf clubs and shoes. (Annoyingly, the practical, Type A side of me was still in the process of learning to go with the flow.)

"Don't worry about it! You bought a ticket to fly down here

on short notice and I'm renting your golf clubs and you're golfing on a course you've never played. Go with it!" I remember
her saying loudly as we laughed and cruised with the top down
in the cool air of San Diego.

"And then we're going to a Padres game afterward, which
is still on your Ballpark Bucket List, right?" Brooke asked
while giggling at the expression on my face.

The expression I wore could best be described as excited,
but with a hint of "How did she pull all this off?" We cruised
around San Diego at night with the top down, the music up
and laughing like we hadn't a care in the world. The fresh air
coming off the Pacific Ocean quickly put me in a relaxed SoCal
state of mind.

Brooke was the main catalyst in planting the seed of hope
in my life at that particular time—and cultivating it—for the
next several months. I consider it a minor miracle to have met
her the way we did and then to have enjoyed all the great times
we were able to share. Sometimes when we find ourselves
lacking the ability to see the positives while going through the
negatives, it takes other people to give us the hope we aren't
able—or willing—to see when dealing with a difficult transition
period in our lives.

This is typical of Brooke. She constantly makes other people happy by doing things she knows will make them smile.
I'd witnessed it with her family on several occasions in the
months after our summer baseball adventures concluded and
she made me smile every time we were together, whether it
was at ballgames or on road trips. She's one of the kindest and
biggest-hearted people I've ever known. Although we weren't
a romantic match, we developed an endearing friendship
throughout those travel adventures.

Brooke was fundamentally important in helping me
through the difficult post-divorce transition period I was going
through. When reflecting on that particular time in my life and

wondering where I would be if Brooke hadn't entered my life makes me even more grateful she had. Sure, I would've been fine overall, but the hope she infused into my life became vital in helping me move forward much sooner than I possibly would have on my own. While cruising around San Diego that night, we discussed plans she'd made for us over the next couple of days. Those times were exciting and entirely unpredictable, and I was starting to get more accustomed to having these experiences in my new life.

MY IDEAL TRIFECTA:
TRAVEL, GOLF AND BASEBALL

My golf partner the next morning was a gentleman by the name of Lamar who was a few years older than me. We had never met, but we got along so well, it felt like we were old college buddies meeting up for a round of golf after several years apart. Between golf shots, we talked about sports, relationships and life. Lamar was a very good golfer, which became clear on the first tee when he drove his ball straight down the middle of the fairway while I pulled mine down the left side—about fifty yards short of his drive. Golf can be extremely frustrating if you let it get to you, but I've learned to take each round as an opportunity to focus on something to improve on.

In golf, as in life, if you're not trying to improve and have some fun, then you're missing the point. Anyone who has played golf will tell you it's a challenging game. It takes lots of practice to play well, which is one reason many people get discouraged and give up the sport. However, if you stick with it and improve, you experience the hope of playing better the more chances you give yourself. (This is another handy metaphor for moving forward in life.) For me, every hole of every round of golf is a new challenge—and opportunity—to improve my game. Golf requires patience by letting go of difficult past holes, focusing on the challenge of the present shot and, finally, enjoying the hope of improving for future rounds. This is why so many books have been written on how golf is an excellent metaphor for life. And also why I truly enjoy playing golf whenever the opportunity opens up.

One of the things I love most about golf is it provides the opportunity to meet people and play on beautiful courses that offer something different at every hole—a lot like life. Golf is challenging whether you're playing against others or yourself. And I've always competed much more with myself than anyone else. When my playing partner(s) play well, I'm genuinely happy for them. I strive to play well every time, but my focus is playing better than the last time I played—not playing better than whomever I'm with. I'm happy golfing the beautiful green courses near home, but I've also been able to play some amazing courses while traveling as a single guy far from home. (Maybe... possibly... probably a metaphor in there about the grass being greener in life.)

"So let me get this straight. You're in San Diego spending time with a *friend*?" Lamar questioned about halfway through our 18 holes together. He gave me a sly smile that I interpreted as if he was saying, "Yeah, right."

"Yep. She's awesome and loves baseball, and we've spent time traveling together going to baseball games in the Midwest and Northwest in the past month or so," I explained as we pulled up to the next tee box.

"Tonight we're heading to a Padres game and then driving up to L.A. on Saturday for my first game at Dodger Stadium." Talking about it made me excited because it was my first trip to watch my team play at Chavez Ravine.

"Ok. But you two are friends and there's no feelings on her end?" he asked, as if wanting to know how the situation played out all summer.

"Honestly, we're just friends. We've spent enough time together to know we're great travel companions. Besides, it's been less than a year since my divorce," I explained after driving the ball and walking back to the golf cart. "And I'm not in any hurry to be back in a relationship, man, especially a long-distance one."

Lamar smiled, then shrugged and said, "Fair enough."

Golf is great for conversation, even if it is interrupted frequently to play the game. Which serves as yet another life metaphor. (Similar to how work is required to "play the game" of life and frequently interrupts the memorable experiences we have throughout the journey.)

"By the way, nice shot," Lamar smiled as I drove the ball down the middle of the fairway. I'd missed the fairway often that day and almost had forgotten what it was like to land where I wanted to.

After making one of a handful of pars I managed that day, we smiled and shook hands on the 18th green—a customary gesture after completing a round of golf. He made several more pars and birdies than me, and I was happy for him. We connected like old buddies, and I genuinely wish I had the chance to golf with Lamar again. As often happens in life, we enter and exit from each other's lives seemingly on a whim. (Look up the definition of the word sonder. It's a great descriptor of our lives, but I didn't realize a word existed that encapsulates how I've felt all these years.) Playing and talking about golf and life that day was a great way of keeping everything in the moment and maintaining perspective.

Admittedly, there had been attraction between Brooke and me that first weekend in Chicago. Looking back, though, I realized it was mainly a result of missing the stability of my previous married life and missing how it felt being in love. The hopeless romantic in me was looking forward to falling in love with the right woman in the future. Eventually I wanted to meet a woman who checked every box on my mental checklist. And it wasn't Brooke's fault that I was still defining what those boxes were at that time.

Initially, she wanted more than friendship from our relationship. As time went on and we spent more time together, it became evident we had much better chemistry as friends. How much of that was due to my state of mind at the time? Who knows? But we all realize things happen in life we can't fully understand at the time. Instead, the reasons become clearer with the wisdom which time and distance provide.

I wasn't in any hurry to get into a serious relationship, especially since there were so many other things I was trying to get figured out. I was still settling into my new living situation, going back to college, changing careers and adjusting to every other aspect of my new life. So while I wasn't falling in love with Brooke, I was loving the fun times—and the *hope* for more fun times—our friendship made possible. But at that time I was still searching for my new self and, diving even deeper, I was searching for self-fulfillment and enduring happiness. I was definitely not searching for a serious relationship or my next wife.

Whether I was home or traveling, some questions were constantly rolling around in my head. Where was I heading in the next chapter of my life? Where did I want to land and begin writing the next chapter? These were only a couple of the seemingly endless questions I was trying to answer. Falling in love with *anyone* at that point was off the table, and it could've taken me down a very different path in life had it been my priority—a direction that would've been adventurous and fun, for sure, but I didn't feel like it would lead to the path of true love or enduring happiness. And it wouldn't have been fair to her or to my own yet-to-be-determined future. As I told Lamar that day while golfing, I openly communicated my feelings with Brooke about where my head and heart were, and we made the most of the times we spent together during those 10 months. I look back with nothing but fond memories, and I believe she does too.

I loved golfing in San Diego that day, and Lamar and I enjoyed each other's company as we navigated our way around the course. We both hit some good shots and some not-so-good shots during the round. (See how easy it is to draw analogies between golf and life?) This trip included travel, golf and baseball, so I was hitting a trifecta of some of the things I absolutely love doing in life. Hope and happiness were making me feel positive about my future chapters.

ENJOYING THE COLLEGE GUY PHASE

It also felt like I was entering a new phase of my post-divorce life—the College Guy phase. I experienced the simple joys of childhood dreams coming true on my first trip to the Midwest in early August. I was now enjoying the in-between period before starting grad school in the spring and ultimately, a new career as an educator. This meant I would eventually have to get back to being an adult and joining the real world again soon.

I realized on this trip—and on several more with Brooke in the months that followed—I was in a special and brief period where I was able to play and enjoy a new normal while it lasted. As with all things in life, I knew this phase would eventually end. After all, the only constant in life is change. So I was determined to ride it out for as long as I possibly could. (If given the chance, wouldn't most of us do the same?)

At the Padres game that night, we were joined by a couple of friends and former coworkers Brooke knew when she lived in San Diego. I conducted my routine pictorial walkabout of the stadium that night, and Petco Park is a gem of a ballpark.

One of my favorite elements includes the way the architects incorporated the old Western Metal Supply brick building into the design and layout of the ballpark down the left field line. It provides a retro feel to the ballyard somewhat reminiscent of Wrigley Field's design to fit amongst the neighborhood affectionately known as Wrigleyville.

As I took my customary trek around the stadium, I talked with fellow baseball fans and took in all the wonderful vantage points the ballpark offers. The stadium, the fans and the weather were all amazing. But a realization hit me that this adventure wouldn't have happened if I was still married. This helped open my eyes to the idea that while divorce discouraged me, it also opened surprising doors I hadn't realized were possible. More importantly, I began embracing the hope that more surprises lay ahead and also the potential for more exciting doors opening where some had closed. This unplanned vacation to SoCal helped me realize my life could be richer—in certain ways—than my previous married life had been. Hope was blossoming.

After the Diamondbacks-Padres game, Brooke and I checked into a posh hotel on Coronado Island. Whether or not you've been to San Diego, Coronado is a must-do. It's home to several relaxed, surfer-vibe bars and eateries. After playing and dunking on the poolside basketball hoop that morning, we went for ice cream at The Del. Coronado is home to the famous Del Coronado Hotel; a beautiful, upscale beachfront property with a wonderful ice cream parlor. Then we moseyed onto the beach for some vitamin D after enjoying the decadent treat. (It's not often we get to use the word *parlor* or *moseyed*. I couldn't resist using them here in much the same way I couldn't resist the ice cream at The Del.)

It was excellent late September weather. Then again, when you're in San Diego, excellent weather is the norm and not the exception. I wanted to enjoy and appreciate everything, especially since I knew there was a clock ticking before starting grad school in the spring. (This was the type of lifestyle a person could easily get used to.) Knowing an abundance of research papers and stress would occupy my life for the next solid year, I indulged in as much of the great food, places and experiences as possible over the next few months with Brooke—and my other friends and family as well.

And that's when I found myself sitting in Dodger Stadium for the first time—another dream come true—while I continued searching for answers to so many post-divorce questions...

DODGER STADIUM

Your first time is always special. This was true of my first trip to Dodger Stadium in Los Angeles. Seeing the ballpark on TV for so many years, I dreamed about stepping foot inside the home of the Dodgers since I was a teenager. The history of the Dodger franchise interested me back then, and I've added to my knowledge base with each passing season. The team left Brooklyn after the 1957 season to the despair of fans in the New York City borough—and to the delight of fans in Los Angeles. The Dodgers played in the L.A. Coliseum for a couple of years before Dodger Stadium was built and opened at Chavez Ravine for the 1962 season. The ballpark is now the third oldest stadium in major league baseball behind Fenway Park in Boston (1912) and Wrigley Field in Chicago (1914). As of this writing, I've been fortunate to watch three games in Fenway, two in Wrigley, and seven in Dodger Stadium... all since my divorce. (Draw whatever conclusions you will from this nugget of information. Go ahead, I don't mind.)

Walking into Dodger Stadium that beautiful fall evening, the sun was beginning to drop into another picture-perfect southern California sunset. I paused while surveying the entire scene. I took in the green field, the light blue hues of the outfield walls, and the darker Dodger Blue hues worn by so many fans. It felt strangely like I was *home* in a place I was visiting for the first time. Once again, Brooke had landed us amazing seats. She knew this occasion was going to be special for me, and she found seats on the third base side, looking directly down the first base line and about 20 rows up from home plate. The truth is we could've sat in the very top row in the farthest spot in the ballpark and I still would've enjoyed the experience immensely. Having seats so close to the field— and my team—was a special bonus, and I must've thanked her a million times during and after the game.

As the national anthem was sung before the game, the tears I wiped away were in appreciation of our military personnel, of course, but also at how fortunate I felt to be standing there at that moment. Despite my best efforts to hide my emotions, I couldn't. Brooke noticed and gave me one of her knowing smiles while the crowd cheered loudly as the anthem concluded. I smiled widely through happy tears and returned my gaze to the field, wiping away the pesky ones trying to escape down my cheeks.

Happy tears are often the reaction to hopes and dreams— both big and small—finally coming true. I had the same reaction my first time in Wrigley Field one month earlier. Hope helped bring me to that moment. It was also about chasing the dream of being happy again—and being able to transcend the emotional changes I was continuing to work through. Indeed, hope is a good thing, especially at times when it's the only thing we have. It's precisely at those times when we fully appreciate the value of believing in our hopes and dreams.

Going to two baseball games in southern California was great. But this was much more meaningful to me than simply enjoying ballgames and checking two more stadiums off my Ballpark Bucket List. Being able to experience my hopes and dreams coming true—and in a relatively short amount of time after my marriage ended—was life changing. Going through a divorce helped me realize I would now be able to pursue some other hopes and dreams—both big and small—in my life. This provided additional hope for what was possible in a future which was literally unfolding in front of me.

"AND NOW IT'S TIME FOR DODGER BASEBALL"

Not long after the game started, I noticed a tall gentleman sitting down near the Dodger dugout on the third base side. I quickly realized it was Magic Johnson, who had become a part-owner of the Dodgers. He also happened to be my childhood basketball idol. And he was about 50 feet down and to the left of where we sat. I had an urge to walk up to him and tell him the same thing millions of people have told him during his NBA career and since he'd retired: "You were my favorite player when I was a kid!" But I didn't. He was trying to enjoy the game and throughout the night, I noticed other people approaching him, which made me glad I refrained from doing so.

I nudged Brooke a time or two and said with a smile, "Even Magic is here supporting my team... no biggie." She laughed as I took in the ballpark and my team playing in front of us.

Early in the game, I looked up to where the legendary Vin Scully was sitting in his booth calling yet another Dodger game in his storied career as a Hall of Fame broadcaster. This was still a couple of years before he retired as the voice of the Dodgers after the 2016 season. Remarkably, Vin Scully had been calling games since he started with the Dodgers in Brooklyn—back in 1950. He was the common bond—the glue for multiple generations of not only Dodger fans, but baseball fans—to the game. Fathers and sons. Moms and sons. Fathers and daughters. Moms and daughters. Grandparents and grandkids. You get the idea. This man has been the singular voice they ALL heard over the years, whether they grew up in Brooklyn or listened to games on the West Coast after the Dodgers left the East Coast.

Long before I stepped foot in Dodger Stadium for the first time, I was listening to Vin Scully call Dodger games. When XM satellite radio became available around 2006, I got a lifetime subscription specifically so I had the option of listening to his voice for any Dodger game, whether traveling or sitting at home. Vin has long been a favorite of Dodger fans and his legacy has been cemented for decades. His signature pregame phrase of "Pull up a chair... It's time for Dodger baseball" is missed by all Dodger fans. One of my hopes from when I was a teenager was to get to watch the Dodgers play in Dodger Stadium and to look up and see Vin Scully broadcasting in the booth. On that night, I checked both items off my list. (Vin Scully passed away in August of 2022 at the age of 94 and will be dearly missed by so many.)

LEGACY. WHAT WILL YOURS BE?

When my younger brothers Dave and Monte mention I was partially responsible for them and their children—my wonderful nieces and nephews—becoming Dodger fans, I get a little choked up. And although my sisters Amy and Amanda aren't big baseball fans, they always let me know when my nieces and nephews have played on Dodger teams in their little league seasons. (As a family, we try not to discuss Amanda's fandom for the Yankees.) Over the years, my awesome siblings have sent pictures of my nieces and nephews in their Dodger caps or shirts, which always make me smile proudly. Knowing that particular part of my legacy—passing on my love of baseball and the Dodgers—has now been solidified and will live on after I'm gone makes me happy inside and out.

As a divorced man without children of my own, I beam with pride knowing I've had an impact on their lives. Hopefully the Dodgers will win a few more championships in my lifetime and theirs. (Then we can even say I had a *positive* impact.) The legacy I will leave behind after departing this earth creeps into my mind more with every passing birthday. We all think about our legacy at some point during our lives. And it means a lot to me that my siblings, nieces and nephews will carry a small part of me with them after I'm gone. By comparison, I realize it's an entirely smaller tribute and legacy than how Dodger fans think of Vin Scully, but it's an honorable tribute and legacy all the same.

BLOSSOMING HOPE

Another type of legacy I'm hopeful of leaving behind is how I've always treated people better than *fairly*. I've tried to treat all people with kindness and respect. Whether close to home or traveling abroad, I've yet to encounter a person who doesn't appreciate being shown kindness and respect. Treating people better than fairly is more rewarding for everyone. By respectfully acknowledging people, we are demonstrating not only kindness, but human-ness. This is why I've tried to take the time to demonstrate kindness and respect to people—whether meeting them for the first time or the 100th. By no means am I always successful, but I feel I've managed to do a solid job of being a positive role model. And it is this legacy of which I am proudest. I'm hopeful—and positive—my amazing nieces and nephews will continue to pass on this legacy of kindness long after I've passed away. Since they are being taught by their amazing parents, I'm happy to report they're all off to a great start.

When I stepped foot in Dodger Stadium for the first time, it had been almost a year since my divorce was finalized. I could not have imagined all of the people, places and things I'd been able to experience in those first 12 months post-divorce. I had found—and been given—hope and had an opportunity to look ahead in life and not dwell on the sadness of my recent past. I started feeling, believing in and sharing hope again. And it was showing signs of blooming fuller than I ever allowed myself to imagine.

"I've learned that people will forget what you said, people will forget what you did, but people will never forget how you made them feel."

- Maya Angelou

75

MINNEAPOLIS, LAS VEGAS AND CANCUN:

Gratitude and Luck

JOURNAL ENTRY (CIRCA 2015)

Hopes and dreams are simultaneously realized and dashed every hour in Las Vegas. Many people go there with the hopes of seeing a show and enjoying the sights and sounds of The Strip and the Fremont Street Experience. And many people go to Vegas with dreams of winning lots of money. I've been to Vegas three times. The first time I visited Sin City was as a married man several years ago. Then a few years later I unexpectedly flew there as a divorcee to spend time with Brooke. I've been there one other time since and enjoyed myself on all three visits.

I've also been ready to head home when my allotted time—and money—was spent. Las Vegas is a city I wouldn't want to live in, but visiting for a few days is fun. Winning large sums of money has eluded me just like it has millions of other people over the years. In Las Vegas, I've been struck by the contrasts between fun and danger, wealth and poverty, and dreaming and losing big. All of these things are on full display and aren't difficult to observe in the desert oasis. Life lessons learned? If you want to dream big, you should be willing to give up a few things—whether your dream comes true or not. In casino games and in life, if you aren't willing to take any risks, you should be willing to accept your chances of winning big—and changing your current and future circumstances—are very unlikely.

For years, Uncle Steve has told me we all create our own luck. I didn't really agree with that sentiment, but began doing so after my divorce. Prior to that, I believed luck simply happened for people and it was always random. I no longer believe this to be true. I feel we can all create—or at least improve—our luck by being grateful and appreciative of the people and experiences in our lives. Saying yes to more opportunities and trying new things can improve our luck as well. Time and again this has been proven to me by the people and places I've experienced before my divorce—but especially since.

I've been incredibly grateful and "lucky" in the couple of years since being at my lowest of lows. Now, I look back and can see some other points Uncle Steve made in the months following my divorce. He said this new chapter could actually be a *happier* chapter than I could imagine and that one day I'd actually be *grateful* for the opportunities divorce provided. It sounded ridiculous at the time. But I understand his perspective now and can honestly say he was correct on both counts.

And that's when I found myself landing in Las Vegas at 4:30 a.m. and entering the code to the hotel suite where I'd be spending the next four nights...

The traveling and fun times with Brooke didn't end with the closing of the baseball season that fall. In fact, they increased much to my pleasant surprise. She made me feel like I deserved these amazing and unpredictable travel adventures at a time when I was questioning my self-worth, especially during the first year after my divorce. I don't have statistical evidence to back up this claim, but I'll go out on a limb and say that 90% of divorcees likely feel a significant drop in their perceived self-worth following a divorce. I will further suggest that many people rush into their first relationship after divorce—and other major life transitions—mainly because they aren't feeling as good about themselves as they should. It's part of being human and how and why it happens is completely understandable. But I was adamant about not letting any kind of rebound relationship—long distance or otherwise—be part of my post-divorce story.

Brooke reminded me it was ok to feel I deserve good things—while traveling and in everyday life—and to pursue living my best life. Back then, I was still processing what my best life was going to look like. In the years since my time with Brooke, I've been living my best life, but I'm continually assessing what my best life looks like going forward. There are aspects of my life I feel can be improved, so searching for ways to upgrade those areas in our lives is important, too. (It's ok if your path isn't well-defined. Focus on what the most important elements are to *you* and things will start taking shape.) Brooke's ability to see things in me when I wasn't able to—during a time I needed to hear it most—helped remind me that we all have a right to good things in our lives. Looking back, she was probably *too* good at it because she was so kind to those around her that I wondered if she spent enough time focusing on herself.

"Do you ever do things for yourself?" I asked her on one of our road trips.

"Sure. I do spa days and stuff like that, but I really enjoy making friends and family happy," she explained while smiling her typically warm smile. That was Brooke being Brooke.

At times, I also worried she might feel I was leading her on by going on travel adventures minus the romantic aspects we shared that first trip I took to the Midwest. But she assured me that wasn't the case.

"Scott, spending time with you is fun for me because you appreciate all of the things we've been able to do together," she would say. "And if I didn't enjoy your company I wouldn't invite you to join me!"

We had several of these exchanges during those 10 months we traveled together. As a result, I learned to allow gratitude to lead the way. Again, feeling and showing gratitude to those we spend time with is vital to creating positivity and making people feel appreciated. We need to continue valuing the people in our lives and the moments we get to spend with them— whether it's for a moment, a season, or a lifetime.

I traveled to Minneapolis a handful of times over the next several months: Brooke's brother's wedding in October, a fishing trip to a cabin in northern Minnesota surrounded by the beautiful colors of autumn, Thanksgiving with her family in Illinois, a Bears-Vikings game (my first NFL game) in December, a crazy January full of surprises, and a fun murder-mystery getaway weekend in Iowa before I started grad school in the spring. We had tons of fun and none of the trips included baseball games or ballparks. (See, I actually *do* travel even if baseball isn't on the itinerary. Granted, it's mostly in the off season, but it does happen.) We had a great time traveling together on every trip mentioned above. And the experiences we had in January further demonstrate the special type of friendship Brooke and I had developed.

WINTER WONDERLAND IN
THE TWIN CITIES

January started with spending a long weekend with Brooke showing me around the Twin Cities—Minneapolis and St.

Paul—in the middle of winter. It was a frozen playland straight out of a Norman Rockwell painting, absolutely beautiful and breathtaking. (And the sub-zero temperatures were breathtaking in a literal way.) In St. Paul we took the Gangster's Tour—an educational trip back in time to the Roaring 20s and Prohibition Era—and walked around Rice Park on a snowy night as families skated at the public outdoor ice rink. Statues there pay homage to famous local authors: Charles Schulz's *Peanuts Gang* and F. Scott Fitzgerald, author of one of my favorite books, *The Great Gatsby*. I enjoyed those trips to the Twin Cities and am looking forward to returning someday. What I don't miss is the icy cold temperatures the region endures throughout winter.

It was 23 degrees below zero in Minneapolis the Monday in early January when I was to fly home—and Brooke was set to fly to Las Vegas for a business conference. Most planes were unable to fly out due to the frosty weather and Brooke's flight was one of only a handful cleared for departure that morning. After texting her about mine being canceled, she quickly walked to my gate and tossed her car and house keys to me before boarding her flight. I appreciated having the option of staying in Minnesota, but had no idea when or if I'd be getting back home on that arctic day.

"Take the Jeep and head back to my place. There's plenty of food and you can stay as long as you want," Brooke texted me before flying to Las Vegas.

This was all very helpful of course, but I'd planned on getting home that night or the next. Neither option was happening. After driving back to her home and searching flights on my laptop throughout the day, it became clear I wouldn't be flying home for at least the next four days.

After Brooke landed in Las Vegas that afternoon, she texted, "Have you tried to transfer your flight to Vegas? You could stay in my suite for the week!"

Suddenly the winter chill of Minneapolis was replaced by thoughts of hanging out in the sunny, 70-degree weather of Las Vegas. I was still getting used to rolling with the changes of my new life. So when I was able to switch my flight later that night—flying to Vegas instead of home—rolling with the changes wasn't terribly difficult to handle. (After all, change can be good, right?)

VEGAS, BABY!

The whole situation of traveling to Minnesota in January and then switching gears and flying to Vegas wasn't something I would've done a mere six months earlier. Since I was decidedly more Type A at that time, I would've likely accepted the situation and stayed in Minneapolis. Yet, there I was, saying yes to an adventure with many unknowns. (And I was starting to embrace this chapter of unpredictability and new experiences in my life.) My flight from the frozen tundra of the north finally took off around 1:30 a.m. I smiled a sleepy, but giddy, smile while reflecting at being in a position to make the most of this new chapter unfolding daily. I was fortunate to be heading to Vegas for the next four days and extremely grateful for the opportunity.

I believe luck and good fortune are both tied directly to gratitude. I've also learned good luck has a way of outweighing bad luck when you focus more on the positive things in life—and less on the negative things. Look, we all have good and bad things happening in our lives. But by focusing more of your energy on the good luck you have, you'll be pleasantly surprised how there tends to be less bad luck. Working hard and making good decisions also helps impact how "lucky" we are, too. (Shocking, right? Who knew?) After all those discussions on the golf course with my Uncle Steve over the years post-divorce, creating our own luck is something I now fully believe in. On the flight, the irony hit me that I was heading to Sin City where people win and lose by how lucky they feel at any given moment. I drifted off on a bumpy nap at 30,000 feet, feeling like I was on a roll. And I hadn't even started gambling yet.

Waking up with the jolt of the plane touching down on the runway, I checked my phone, and it was 4:30 a.m. local time. Knowing she'd be sleeping by the time I arrived from Minneapolis, Brooke texted me the entry code to her suite located in an upscale hotel off The Strip. I drowsily plopped into a cab after grabbing my luggage and was surprised at how busy Vegas was even at that time. Rubbing my sleepy eyes as the cab cruised by the MGM Grand, the fake Eiffel Tower, and the beautiful Bellagio fountains, I smiled wearily and thought, "Vegas, baby."

I took the elevator to the expensive—and expansive—suite and quietly let Brooke know I'd made it safely. She whispered she'd try not to wake me in an hour when she'd be getting ready for the day. I was so tired, I didn't even hear her when she left that morning. In the daylight, the suite was more spacious than I realized. Having only slept a few choppy hours on the plane and in the room, I stepped into the walk-in shower— apparently built to hold 10 people—and remembered soaking in the warm water for several minutes. While standing there rinsing the chilly northern temperatures away, I giggled about the unexpected turn of events I was experiencing.

Not even 24 hours had passed since Brooke and I were in separate lines to board planes in busy and frozen Minneapolis. And now I was leisurely showering in an upscale, high-rise hotel in Las Vegas. It all had a surreal, movie-like feel. I was looking forward to enjoying Vegas during the day and hanging out with Brooke at night for the rest of the week. I was happy— and comfortable—being there under entirely unpredictable circumstances. Sometimes growth takes place when you least expect it.

After showering, I came to the realization that all I had packed were warm clothes for the frigid weather of the Upper Midwest. Las Vegas was never in the plan. Indeed, many things that had happened in the past year since divorce—both good and bad—were never in the plan either. Making the most of the opportunities as they arose was one thing I kept reminding myself during my first year post-divorce. By maintaining a positive attitude, things have a tendency of working out. Making the most of how things work out—even when it's less than ideal—is also important in moving forward. This mindset also helps us improve our own luck. When you start seeing certain things as opportunities to thrive rather than opportunities to complain, it's remarkable how much you notice situations tend to go your way. Trusting this to be true takes a lot of time and faith. I wish I'd learned this lesson earlier in life. (How many times do we all wish for this?) I continued reminding myself every experience and opportunity brings us to our current situation.

Knowing my time in the College Guy phase would be ending in a few months helped me agree to Brooke's idea of switching my flight to Vegas. I'm glad I didn't fall back into the safe and boring decision of not flying to Sin City. The previous version of me would've been nervous about the sudden switch in plans. But the new version of me was happy to be there—having a great suite didn't hurt either—and spending the next four days in sunny weather instead of being stuck alone in frozen Minneapolis. (Convenient metaphor: focusing on the warmth in life helps us feel less of the dreariness.) During the first day in town, Brooke texted and asked if I wanted to go to dinner with some of her colleagues while I was in Vegas. Dinner the next evening was planned for one of Wolfgang Puck's restaurants. It was more of a rhetorical question since she already knew I'd say yes. (Again, how could I pass up that opportunity?)

Venturing out that first afternoon in Vegas, I withdrew a small amount of money from an ATM and decided when it was gone, it was gone. Going back for more funds was not an option, which had less to do with having strong willpower and more to do with the very limited funds in my bank account. I walked to the aptly-named Wynn Casino and won $150 on a slot machine. Obviously, I was very happy about the unexpected win. Indeed, my luck was improving—on that trip and in general.

Roulette has long been my favorite casino game, and although I lost some money playing at the tables that day, I knew risking all of my slot winnings on roulette would be a bad decision. Instead, I decided to buy a couple shirts at the mall near the hotel so I wouldn't be wearing sweaters all week—and I also had money left over for lunches the next few days—and a little bit to gamble with. (So you might say it was a Wynn-win. My apologies. I'll try to limit the awful puns.)

Brooke texted that afternoon with the time and location of dinner for the next night since we didn't know if we'd be seeing each other before then. Being an extrovert, I was looking forward to meeting Brooke and her colleagues while enjoying a great meal. And the three-hour dinner, drinks and conversation the following night turned out to be exceptional. (It's still the most expensive steak I've ever ordered.) We all laughed so much that night, it felt like I had known everyone at the table for years instead of hours. It's a great memory that still pops into my mind now and then. However, my best memory from that week in Vegas was a happy coincidence the first full night I was there.

STILL ON A ROLL

My mom and stepdad planned a vacation in Arizona that January, but I couldn't remember when they were starting their trip. They were snowbirds in training, since only Mom was fully retired then. So I called her and explained how I'd ended up in Vegas. Mom excitedly said they'd be spending one night in Vegas on their way to Arizona and would be arriving that first evening I was in town. The timing was perfect, so we made plans to meet up and I treated them to dinner. Spending time with them was unexpected, and I'm glad we made the most of it. Brooke wasn't able to join us due to a prior commitment with a client. (Unlike me, she was in town on business after all.) Before dinner—as a surprise bonus—Mom and Roger said they'd already planned to loan me some money since I had come to Vegas without much money. They knew I'd be grateful for their kindness, and I absolutely was.

Shortly after they arrived, the three of us decided to gamble a little before dinner. I'm glad we did because I won $200 at the slot machines before sitting down to eat. (I was still on a roll, baby!) Roulette was a losing proposition for me that trip, but fortunately the slots kept me "in the money." The winnings and that night's payout funded more gambling and meals the next couple days before I flew home. Naturally, I was still very much enjoying the College Guy phase.

Knowing my time spent in that phase would soon end, I was riding it out as long as possible. (Vegas rule: you don't interrupt a "heater.") Getting to spend time with my mom and stepdad was truly the icing on the cake to that unplanned time in Las Vegas. I was grateful and happy for everything, including the sub-zero temperatures in Minneapolis which set the entire change of plans in motion. And it wasn't lost on me that the whole Vegas experience wouldn't have been possible if I had decided to stay home—or in Minneapolis—rather than choosing to say yes and "spread my wings and fly" when I had the opportunity.

And that's when I found myself sitting on a beach in Cancun sipping pina coladas only a week after escaping frozen Minneapolis and soaking up the bright lights and good times in Las Vegas...

The first three weeks of January began unlike any new year I'd ever experienced. Brooke and I had planned a Cancun trip prior to our *unplanned* Vegas extravaganza, which had come on the heels of our frozen winter wonderland adventures around the Twin Cities. For several years, Brooke had taken one of her friends to Cancun to an all-inclusive resort for a week of fun and relaxation. (See what I'm talking about? She was like this long before I came into the picture.) I was fortunate to be the chosen friend that year. She knew I'd be starting grad school in a few months and generously made the trip happen with very minimal financial obligation on my part.

When I resisted initially, she explained that each of her friends had been treated to the same deal in previous years, which made me feel better about accepting her invitation. (Can you visualize the arm twisting? So painful.) Only a week after getting home from freezing Minnesota and sunny Vegas, I was heading back to Minneapolis for one night before flying to Cancun. And to think *all* of this came about after accidentally meeting Brooke on Words With Friends a mere six months earlier. (Yes, I still shake my head and smile in disbelief.)

My first trip to Mexico and the resort city of Cancun was everything I hoped for and more. Mornings were spent enjoying breakfast overlooking the beautiful blue ocean waves. Lunches were savored while overlooking the beautiful blue-green ocean waves followed by late afternoons lounging on a beach cot with a continuous supply of vitamin D and pina coladas. (As you can imagine, it was a busy schedule, but we strictly adhered to it.) Occasionally, we'd mix it up by wading in the bathtub-warm waters of the Caribbean and then lazily catching more rays with the ocean breezes cooling us down. (Napping was encouraged but completely optional, of course.) Dinners were spent enjoying great conversation and delicious seafood and authentic Mexican food—my personal favorite—while overlooking the ocean and picture-perfect sunsets.

CREATING OUR OWN LUCK

Being there was amazing, especially in January, when the temperatures were an ideal blend of cooler nights and low 80s during the days. It was my first time ever having a sunburn in the middle of winter. (But somehow it didn't hurt as much as any of the summer sunburns I'd had in my life.) I loved everything about the experience, and it was difficult to leave, especially since I knew this was the unofficial end to the College Guy phase I had been enjoying for the past six months. Nothing lasts forever—good or bad—so being able to appreciate every phase in our lives is vital to making the most of the time we have. Again, when looking back on all of these amazing adventures, I had helped create my own luck by being openly grateful and appreciative of the people and opportunities presented to me. I also said yes to many of the opportunities that presented themselves. Some doors had definitely closed, but many, many more were opening ahead of me as I continued my journey forward.

"You can't go back and change the beginning,
but you can start where you are and change the ending."

 – *C.S. Lewis*

BOISE:

Grad School and Life's Many Paths

JOURNAL ENTRY (CIRCA 2017)

Rebooting my life has been equal parts frustrating and rewarding. Looking back on the past few years, I've totally rebooted my life at mid-life. I've completed an intense grad school program, started a new career and am adjusting to a new financial reality. I'm completely comfortable living alone, which is something I wouldn't have expected to feel a couple years ago. Now I'm at a point where I'm ready to find a companion and hopefully fall madly in love. But I'm finding the process frustrating and even laughable at times. Obviously I'm not the only person to go through these life transitions. There are millions of people around the country and the world that have taken similar paths. But to say restarting my life has been *challenging* is an understatement.

Honestly, I'm completely grateful for all of the amazing travel opportunities and people which have been added to my life, especially post-divorce. But I can't shake the feeling that grad school interrupted the positive momentum which had been building that first year or so after my divorce. I'm still unsure if grad school was the right decision. It's been almost two years since I completed the program and became an edu-cator. So time will tell. In some ways, I feel like it was the right decision, but not so much in other ways.

Landing a job as a teacher at the high school I'd hoped for has obviously been a huge positive. But the job of teaching has been more stressful and requires working consistently more hours per week than any job I've previously held. The business model of public education is problematic, which is nothing surprising or new. The salary in education, especially in states like Idaho, leaves much to be desired. Although the pay (or lack thereof) isn't why I decided to become an educator, the constantly rising costs of everything else compared to teacher pay doesn't help how I feel. The biggest upside about becom-ing a teacher has been the students and parents with whom I've had the opportunity to build relationships.

These wonderful connections have been extremely mean-ingful in so many ways and are what truly make the profession so fulfilling. The interactions with my students, whether while learning, laughing, or having serious discussions, have been so memorable and are especially important to me. Many stu-dents and parents have told me I've made a big difference in their lives, and *that* is something I've never had with any pre-vious job. And it means more to me than I can truly express.

And that's when I found myself meeting a woman during my first real attempt at online dating and feeling like there was potential until...

BACK TO SCHOOL

Several friends and family members encouraged me to pursue a career in education after the divorce, and I wanted a fulfilling career which allowed some flexibility to travel. Teaching offered a path to both. Becoming an educator required certification, and going back to school meant I'd be returning for a third time. I never imagined my career path would include three separate ventures into college. Right out of high school, I worked hard for five years and earned a marketing degree with honors—funded mostly by academic scholarships I earned with my high school and college GPAs—of which I'm very proud. A few years after graduating—while working full-time at an international corporation with a branch office in downtown Boise—I pursued a history degree by earning six credits per semester for the next three and a half years. I didn't take courses during the summers because I wanted to drop back to 40-hour work weeks and have some semblance of work/life balance again. The most recent stint in school was a year and a half after divorce, when I decided to pursue a graduate certification in education and teach high school history. I felt like my life was at a crossroads then. In some ways, I still do.

When I was still married, I enjoyed being a part-time substitute teacher at some of the local schools while I was trying to establish myself as a freelance writer. Subbing consistently at the same junior high and high schools allowed me to get to know the students and teachers fairly well. Students would often ask why I wasn't a *real* teacher, which I took as a compliment since teens aren't known for being overly kind to subs. Fortunately, classroom management and connecting with students wasn't difficult for me. Any educator can tell you there's a big difference between being a sub and being a teacher when it comes to the rest of the job, however. The time spent by teachers on lesson planning and grading is a major reason why the profession requires so many additional work hours on weekends and before and after the eight-hour school day ends.

As a sub, many educators encouraged me to become a teacher while I was married and continued to do so after I divorced. I continued forging ahead as a part-time sub and freelance writer for about a year or so while continuing to process the end of my marriage. Growing up, I never pictured myself as a teacher, but my new reality forced me to adjust my mindset to being flexible to different paths for my future. (I was learning how vital this idea was to moving forward in life.) Although not completely convinced a career in education was for me, I decided to pursue the profession, since it felt like growing to love the job was possible. And also because I needed a more consistent income than the part-time freelance writer and sub jobs were providing. It's no secret how economic circumstances—both fortunately and unfortunately—can have a lasting impact on our career paths and other life path decisions as well.

I look back on some of my career, relationship and life decisions and wonder how things might've been if I'd been able to make different decisions under improved economic circumstances. (I'm betting this sounds familiar to nearly everyone reading this book.) The decision I made when going back to school, for example, required a ridiculously large amount to be borrowed via student loans. The issue was compounded when I learned that in this particular graduate program we were told holding a job—even 10 hours per week—would not be sustainable during the intense year-long program. (And I found out the hard way they were right.) If I'd been 25 when I completed the program and had more time to make up for the lower starting wages and higher-than-anticipated student loan amounts, then some of these financial woes could've been mitigated. But I wasn't 25 at the time, and I'm far from that age now. Lesson learned.

GRAD SCHOOL BLUES

When I started grad school, I knew my travel opportunities would be limited. This forced me to adjust my paths to traveling for the year I was in school. Realizing the new normal amount of travel I'd been experiencing wasn't realistic while returning to school made it necessary to be more creative. So I began taking day trips since longer road trips were not an option. During a time when my stress level was rising and my income was falling at equally alarming rates, I'd drive to the mountains on Saturdays and not do the readings and papers I should've been working on. As a result, Sundays often became full workdays, too. But I intentionally tried using Saturdays as the one day every week I could take my mind off school. One of my happy places is the town of McCall situated around a beautiful mountain lake just two hours north by car from where I live. I've been going all my life and spent many Saturdays there during grad school recharging my batteries. It was my place to breathe, relax and keep things in perspective. And it still is. (BBQs and laughing with my Uncle Monte, who lives in a nearby town, were and are good for the soul.)

Creative budgeting was nothing new to me, but going back to school as a single guy required a new level of fiscal responsibility. Again, I learned student loans could only be stretched so thin. (And winning millions in the lottery continued to elude me—as it continued to elude millions of others.) Naturally, I questioned my decision of going back to school and beginning a new career at my age. I had taken a leap of faith to explore new paths to travel after my divorce, and it helped me grow as a person. By choosing the back-to-school path toward a new career, I took another leap of faith. This new path obviously wasn't as much fun as my recently concluded phase and the amazing travel opportunities I'd experienced. Being open to change was a required post-divorce mindset, and it's continually helped me grow.

During the intense year-long grad program, I typically ate many hurried meals of ramen, spaghetti or cold pizza alone by the kitchen sink while watching the last few minutes of a ballgame—before working on my next research paper that was due. Overall, it was not a fun period in my life. I continually reminded myself to take everything in stride and focus on my future. Having no guarantee of a job upon graduating from the program and feeling stuck with few traveling opportunities drove me crazy at times that year. Fortunately, this new career path came with the perk of having more time off to travel than my previous jobs. (This thought pushed me more than I should admit, but it's the truth.) But I also worked more hours during that year of grad school—and each of the first several years of teaching—that my summer downtime was more than fully earned. Having travel goals helped me focus when times were especially stressful and lonely. (Which meant I focused on traveling a lot.)

All the required sacrifices—late nights studying, working on countless research papers and projects, long days in the classroom, 4-hour nights of sleep, passing up time with family and friends—had me questioning whether it would all be worthwhile. When I was lacking quality sleep and felt over-stressed—which was often—friends reminded me life has multiple paths and chapters. Discovering some old doors and paths were shut meant facing the truth that some were closed for good. (At times, realizing that this was a *good* thing took a little more time than I wanted.) Several times during that year I recognized the need to adjust my outlook toward new career and relationship opportunities in my present. It also meant looking forward to the unknown doors and paths which would be opening in the future.

Going back to college for a third time felt like I was starting over in my career—and in life. But I look back on my grad school chapter with gratitude for the people I met and some of the limited travel opportunities it provided. Finishing the grad program resulted in landing a job teaching U.S. history at the high school where I'd hoped to begin my new career path. This made going back to grad school worthwhile—for the most part—since finding happiness in a relationship continued to be elusive. In the process I learned to try reframing the transition periods—in our careers, relationships and lives—as *opportunities* to choose new paths we may not have previously considered. Staying positive and looking forward to the things that make us happy is a great way to maintain focus and hope while our new doors and paths are opening up. Embracing this mindset can be challenging, but it's completely worth doing so in the long run.

FEELING DISCONNECTED

In the period between getting divorced and going back to college, I didn't have time for dating. During grad school—when it felt like I had to schedule time for everything, including sleep—I met a couple women I was interested in but had scarcely little time and money to pursue dating. So after completing the grad program, I decided it was time to jump into the online dating pool. Keeping an open mind to multiple paths also applied to being open to meeting new women and potential romantic opportunities as well.

Getting back into dating was more than a little awkward for me. I hadn't been on a date since the 1990s. Let that sink in for a moment, because it definitely made me pause more than once. After spending so many years as a married man, I had no idea how to go about meeting women. During the process of dating, there were times that gave me hope of meeting someone who checked all the boxes. (At other times it made me question what the hell I was doing.) But putting myself out there provided the opportunity to meet new people and experience new things, so I went with it.

A lot had changed in the dating world during the years I was married. Online dating transformed from a stigmatized into a normalized way of meeting people. Filling out my first profile on a dating site felt odd and superficial. Even selecting photos I was happy with—I have a tendency to close my eyes for pictures—was a chore, and I quickly realized that while I was willing to give it a chance, online dating was awkward. And some of the dates made me feel even more uncomfortable as I questioned the value of trying the online route. (I'm sure many of you have had similar experiences and can totally relate.) But I went with it for a little while because I was missing female companionship and was adjusting to how the modern world of dating worked.

When I told a couple of my married female friends that I was ready to find someone to spend more time with on a regular basis, they cautioned me not to expect too much from online dating. So I lowered my expectations about the potential of finding true love online. They knew I was ready to meet someone who'd check the boxes of my prerequisite parameters of potential partners. (That alliteration is for my English language loving friends. You know who you are.) After a few dates with women I'd connected with online, I felt disconnected and started missing the days of organically meeting someone in public or being introduced by a friend of a friend.

Since my previous dating days ended at 21, it wasn't like I had tons of experience in that area even when I was a young, single guy. I've always been a hopeless romantic who enjoys a good rom-com and believed in the right person coming along for each of us. And I'm still a hopeless romantic, but I no longer subscribe to the idea of having just *one* right person. Instead, I believe in the possibility of several during our lifetimes—depending on life circumstances, of course. We have to be in a place—physically and mentally—of being open to the possibilities of meeting said people.

ONLINE DATING BLUES

About six months after divorcing, I'd briefly tried online dating, and it was fueled by loneliness and desperation. It was a bad combination, and the results were equally awful. I went on a couple of dates and immediately knew we weren't going to be a good match. But I also met a couple of women back then with whom I'm still friends. That was the single best thing about my first experience with online dating.

Over two years passed before I tried online dating again. After grad school, I was in a much healthier mindset. I was still a little lonely, but I was no longer desperate. I had lowered my expectations based on my previous experiences, but my mental checklist—and high standards—remained intact. Over the years, I've been asked by friends if there's room for flexibility on my checklist. Of course there is—for the right person. I'd met a few women that I instantly knew weren't what I was looking for and the boxes weren't even close to being checked. No second dates happened. But then I went on a date with a woman who seemingly had real potential on the box-checking scale.

MAYBE... POSSIBLY A GOOD CATCH?

She was intelligent, attractive and funny. Meeting up at a downtown brewpub, we enjoyed a couple glasses of wine with dinner as we got to know each other. The date was going so well the hopeless romantic in me started to wonder if maybe, just maybe, this could lead to a second date and perhaps more.

After talking about our backgrounds and the requisite talk about our exes, we walked around downtown hand-in-hand and it felt good to be on a date with someone I was increasingly interested in going on a second date with. She seemed to feel the same. After wandering around and ending up at her car, we kissed and agreed that a second date would happen soon. For the first time in the strange, new online dating world I was adapting to, there was hope in finding someone I genuinely wanted to pursue. It was exciting and gave me some butterflies inside.

She explained her job required frequent business trips, and she mentioned this had been an issue in previous relationships. I remember telling her it was great because I had a very busy life as well and was not in a hurry to be in a serious relationship. She breathed a sigh of relief and said she felt the same. The next morning we texted each other our mutual feelings that the night before had been wonderful. We planned our second date in a week or two after she was supposed to return from her business trip. Apparently, the business trip went really well because that was the last time I heard from her. (So, yeah, my first promising post-divorce date went well... until it didn't.) Hope dashed. Frustration returned. Back to the drawing board.

ONLINE DATING LESSONS LEARNED

There were positives I took away from the experience though. First, I was reminded that people flake out for reasons we'll never know, so taking it personally is a pointless exercise, even though I still did for a moment. Second, meeting up for coffee versus dinner during this dating chapter of my life was much less time consuming—and less expensive—and made more sense, especially if one ends up dating often. I went on enough dates over the course of that year that coffee dates made sense from a time and monetary standpoint. As a person who has always connected well with others, I'm blessed—and cursed—by knowing early in the process of dating whether I will vibe well with someone.

Again, coffee dates are great for this reason since they don't last as long as dinner dates unless, of course, you want them to. In fact, during my online dating experience I didn't seek a second date from anyone. (When you know, you *know*.) Others have asked how I can be so sure about someone after one date. My simple and honest answer is that unless she gives me butterflies and makes me smile without realizing it, then I know she's not the one I want to spend more time with. (Some of you know exactly what I'm talking about while others are shaking their heads. I smile at both sets of people, but for vastly different reasons.) Going forward, I added a new box to my mental checklist: I want a woman who makes me smile, but also one who makes me laugh. Unfortunately, this quality has been more difficult to find than expected.

There's nothing wrong with a person who wants to have that feeling of falling in love for the first time again and who knows when there's potential and—more importantly—when there's not. The former is worth spending time and money on. The latter is not. Love isn't easily quantified, and it's different for everyone since we're all looking for different things and are at different phases in our lives. (And, admittedly, I've always been a picky bastard.) There are times I've considered lowering the expectations bar, but I've been fortunate to have dated women in recent years who helped keep that bar high without compromising my standards. Two of them happened to live in cities which were several states away from mine. Neither of those relationships lasted past six months. Long distance relationships can be good at times, but not so much at others.

Online dating taught me a few key things. Number one lesson learned was that dating today is much different, and I needed to adapt. Number two lesson learned was it was ok to meet and have nothing in common and still find interesting people to stay in contact with. Even if it didn't lead to anything even remotely close to romance, it felt good to be connecting with new women and getting a chance at seeing things from different perspectives.

FINDING NEW PATHS

Realizing new career and dating paths were opening up was exciting because I allowed myself to embrace the possibilities of new doors appearing ahead of me. Some people understandably have a difficult time getting over the fact that some doors are closed permanently behind them. Many years after my parents divorced, my father still couldn't seem to overcome their divorce. After getting divorced, I empathized—and truly understood—Dad's pain more than I had while he was still alive.

Since the divorce came about four years after he passed away, we weren't able to have a discussion on the topic. Naturally, I would've told him how much more I understood his perspective after going through one. I also would've explained how I understood Mom's perspective much more as well. Determined not to take the same path as my father, I made a conscious decision to acknowledge the doors which were closed behind me and to look forward to my future paths. In order to move forward, we have to develop new perspectives on the past. Being open to unplanned doors opening and having a growth mindset to actually walk through those doors can be exciting if you allow it to be. Getting out there and saying yes to new opportunities—whether traveling or meeting up with people locally—and *living* is the best way we can move forward.

The most important thing I learned in my post-grad school venture into dating was it was ok to look for my next love—both online and organically—but it was even more important to realize I was no longer dependent on any one person to make me happy. I had become more independent—out of circumstance and necessity—in those first few years after divorcing. And I was about to embark on a solo road trip across the country that helped me value my independence and feel more freedom than I ever realized—or imagined—was possible.

"Not all those who wander are lost."

– *J.R.R. Tolkien*

BOSTON TO BOISE:

Replacing One with Many

JOURNAL ENTRY (CIRCA 2017)

Looking back on the first several months following the divorce, I remember telling myself that 'transcending' was the way to get through the seemingly endless waves of emotions I was dealing with daily. So I tried to rise above my situation and keep a positive perspective. Friends and family reminded me things would get better, which helped me keep the big picture in mind that this, too, would pass. But when you're going through any major life transition, it's much easier said than done.

Back when seemingly everything in my life was changing, I continually reminded myself good things were going to come my way again. It gave me hope—however fleeting and distant—which I clung to when I was struggling through those darkest days early on. Within the first couple of years postdivorce, feeling depressed and lost in the shuffle began being replaced by hope and finding direction by connecting with so many new friends and traveling to so many new places.

Reflecting on the five years since getting divorced, meeting and spending time with so many people helped smooth over the road ahead. I'm truly grateful to each person in this group, which includes family, old and new friends, and former and current students. By reconnecting with some family and friends I'd lost touch with while married, it helped ground me and served as a good reminder that things would eventually get better. Developing connections with the new people that came into my life post-divorce helped me understand good things were in my present and my future as well.

And that's when I found myself unexpectedly driving from Boston to Boise only a few days after returning home from a weekend in Austin...

Shortly after completing the year-long grad school program, my younger brother Dave and I took a road trip to Seattle. Summertime in Seattle is tough to match for its beauty and the way it cools down quickly when the sun begins setting across Elliott Bay. Watching sunsets from the waterfront or from the ballpark never gets old. Seattle is a seven-hour drive and also home to our closest major league baseball team—the Mariners—and Dave and I had such a good time we decided to take a similar trip the following summer.

On both trips we spent a night with Mom, who lived in the beautiful farmland of Eastern Oregon at the time. We were welcomed by the pleasant scents of the alfalfa and mint fields in the summer air as we arrived at our mom and stepdad's house. Crickets, cows and coyotes could be heard into the night as we drifted off to sleep after enjoying dessert with Mom on those peaceful summer evenings. As always, we loved spending time catching up with our mom, and—whether we were spending a night or a week—the door was always lovingly open. The next morning we hopped back on the road to continue our journey to watch a Mariners game and spend time sightseeing in Seattle. My brother and I enjoyed all of these things but, more importantly, those road trips provided time for reminiscing about our childhoods, sharing laughs and creating more memories together. It was the type of stuff all good journeys—especially road trips—should include.

After driving all day from Seattle—and only 15 minutes after arriving back in Boise—I missed a putt to win a new car in a contest held on the 18th hole at a local, private golf course. Earlier in the week, I was one of a handful of people to have made a 20-foot qualifying putt to have an opportunity of winning the car on Sunday. The private club hosts the Boise Open every year and is a minor tour stop for future PGA golfers. Missing the putt of 30+ feet didn't bother me—even with a crowd of maybe a hundred people watching—because I was grateful Dave and I enjoyed our trip and still made it home from Seattle so I could even *attempt* the putt. (Winning a $250 gift card didn't hurt my feelings either.) Opportunity doesn't always lead to great things, but it can if you're open to taking chances that put you in a position to do so.

IT'S OK TO MESS WITH TEXAS

I flew to Texas a few days after my brother and I returned home from Seattle. Having planned the trip to Austin a few months earlier, it was my first trip to visit my cousin Megan, her husband Brian, and their daughter Mckenzie. We took in a Round Rock Express ballgame, played Top Golf and ate delicious Texas BBQ and laughed all weekend. (As you can see, traveling might become an addiction.) This would be the first of several trips I took to Austin over the next year and a half. And I've loved being in Austin the other half-dozen times I've been able to visit as well. The summer heat and humidity took some getting used to, but the great times and laughter shared with family and my friend Ryon in the great city of Austin are always wonderful no matter what time of year I'm there. Whether flying or driving, I truly cherish all the trips I've been fortunate to take in my life so far. And the ones spent with family will always have a special place in my heart.

As I was flying home from Austin after that trip in early August, I was reflecting on what a great summer it had been. In June, I'd visited my wonderful friends Kyle and Shelea in Portland on my way to the Oregon Coast—a tradition we started several years ago when we were new friends right after I got divorced. Then came a road trip to Seattle in July with Dave a few days before flying to Austin. Since traveling isn't free, I had to creatively plan and finance my way through the year—as I do every year—especially having school loans to pay off once again. As I've mentioned before, traveling on a budget can be done—and still be fun. There are some great online travel sites which help cut costs if you spend a little time researching. (Having cool friends that find amazing travel deals helps, too.)

Of course, some travel opportunities pop up unexpectedly, and planning in advance isn't always an option. Which is why I constantly suggest going when you can, while you can. I'm not opposed to putting flights and hotels on my credit card and paying them off in future months. Going into debt to travel is worth it—as long as you don't go overboard. (I have never regretted using my credit card for travel opportunities, and I don't suppose I ever will.) Waiting to travel when retirement arrives has some advantages, but life is too short to put off everything until we reach retirement. I've listened and witnessed far too many cautionary tales of those who've waited till retirement age to start enjoying life. Each and every time I have heard a variation of the same moral of the story: enjoy life along the way, and don't wait till the end to begin doing so.

Landing back in Boise after a weekend in Austin, I remember thinking my fun summer of travel was over, but my summer was actually about to get even better.

WHEN OPPORTUNITY KNOCKS, OPEN THE FREAKIN' DOOR!

I checked my phone after landing and saw a text from Kerry, my next-door neighbor at the time. She asked if I wanted to go have dinner and mentioned an idea she wanted to discuss. I dropped my bags at home without unpacking and we headed to a favorite Mexican food place in Boise. At dinner, Kerry and I talked about my recent trips to Seattle and Austin and her trip to Boston. I lamented summer being nearly over and I was starting my first job in education in less than two weeks.

Kerry is originally from Boston—we met when she moved next door earlier that summer—and worked as a traveling nurse at one of the two primary hospitals in town. She recently flew back to Boise after visiting her family and friends in Boston while I was still in Austin. And she had a dilemma. That's when she pitched her idea to me. She originally planned on driving back across the country from Boston, but her car was being repaired and still wasn't fixed by the time she needed to be back to work. So she flew back to Boise instead. Knowing my love for travel, Kerry asked if I'd be willing to fly to Boston and then drive her car back across the country by myself. She proposed we split the cost of my flight to Boston, and she'd pay for gas since she'd already budgeted to do so when she was back East. After taking exactly a half second to think about it, I had two questions before I said yes.

The first question was whether I could watch a few Major League Baseball games—and thus check more ballparks off my

Bucket List—along my route across America. The second question was if I could use 10 days to complete the trip. That was exactly how many days of summer I had left. Had she answered with a no to either question, I would've still said yes to the trip, but not having to hurry home was icing on the proverbial (travel) cake. Kerry said yes to both questions, and we immediately pulled out our phones and started looking at major league team schedules along my proposed route as we finished dinner.

We determined there were four major league games I could realistically attend along the route and also the Baseball Hall of Fame in Cooperstown, New York—a place I'd wanted to visit since I was a teen. To say I was excited would be a tremendous understatement. (How could anyone NOT be excited for this opportunity?) Saying yes more and being open to new travel opportunities has yielded so many unexpected adventures in my post-divorce life.

After dinner and while processing the trip at home later that night, I laughed out loud at the fortunate turn of events. On the flight home from Austin earlier that day, I'd daydreamed how to possibly fit one more adventure in but never imagined *this* type of trip would happen. I now had an opportunity for one more adventure before summer ended and my first job in education began. Including the road trip to Seattle with my brother—and then the road trip from Boston to Boise—I drove from coast to coast in the span of a few weeks. I was aware at the time I may never have the opportunity to do so again. (Obviously, I would love to repeat the trip, but it hasn't happened... yet.) Three days later, while boarding my flight to Boston, I felt a bit nervous but also more excited than for any trip I'd taken in my life. I'd never driven across the country—solo or otherwise—but getting out of my comfort zone had me feeling much more confident than fearful.

One of the greatest aspects of traveling has always been

the change of scenery and sense of freedom it offers. The ability to leave behind some of the daily stresses of work and life—to varying degrees—is a huge reason I love traveling both near and far. The opportunities to see and do new things is exciting and good for the soul.

A few years prior to taking the trip, I'd completely let go of the last remnants of negativity regarding the divorce. By the time I took my cross-country journey, I was so much happier *not* being married. Never did I feel as independent and free—in my entire life—as when I was able to fly to Boston and begin my solo road trip across America back home toward Boise.

BOSTON: MORE THAN A FEELING

I was fortunate to have visited Boston twice before taking my epic solo road trip on my third time there. The first trip happened about five years before the divorce when my ex-wife and I traveled to Ireland and spent time in Boston before flying to drive around the Emerald Isle. We spent another night in Boston before flying back to Boise upon returning to the States. The Red Sox were getting ready for the playoffs that season (2007) and we were able to take a Fenway Park Tour and watch the eventual World Series Champions take batting practice while we were atop the Green Monster ("The Monstah" if you hear it in the local accent). It was a dream come true to be inside historic Fenway Park that trip, but I still wanted the true baseball fan experience of being there for an actual game. Little did I know it would take eight years before I was able to return to Boston.

My second trip to Boston came right after finishing my grad school program when a friend pledged to take me to Boston and Fenway Park as a graduation present. Despite pleading with her that it was much too generous a gift—which

Stephanie continually assured me it wasn't—a trip was planned. Literally the day before we were supposed to fly across the country, she called me saying she wouldn't be able to go because of an issue at work. As bummed as we both were, Stephanie urged me to go alone since she knew how much going to Fenway meant to me. (Yes, I fully realize I'm fortunate to have some pretty amazing friends.)

So I flew alone—which I had done many times before—but this was the farthest from home I'd ever traveled by myself. (I felt like Frodo Baggins leaving the Shire. Ok, maybe not quite the same, but it's a convenient opportunity to throw in a *Lord of the Rings* reference for those that appreciate such things.) On my second trip to Boston, I spent five days finding my way around Boston and getting to know a city I'd wanted to visit again. Although I wished Stephanie had been able to join me as planned, it was still a great week touring Boston. Among other things, I loved visiting the Harvard campus, walking among the historical sites downtown, and basically soaking up the coolness of the city overall. The blending of old architecture with the new—often on the same block—makes my inner historian side happy and, of course, my Irish roots beam with pride when I'm in Boston.

"SWEET CAROLINE... GOOD TIMES NEVER SEEMED SO GOOD"

The main reason for taking my second trip to Beantown, of course, was to watch a Red Sox game in Fenway Park. And since I was alone on that trip and love baseball, I watched games on consecutive nights. (When in Rome, right?) Of course, as is my custom when visiting a ballpark for the first time, I explored and chatted with fans all around Fenway before and during both games. One guy I hung out with for most of the game on the second night had possibly the coolest job in the country. He was a high school P.E. teacher from San Diego. I half-jokingly asked him if all of his classes were spent outside in the 75-degree and sunny weather or if he actually had to stay indoors once or twice during the school year. He laughed and said he had no complaints. With the time I spent that week in Boston, I could totally relate.

After flying home from that trip, some people asked if I'd felt lonely going by myself. Not at all. My mom and Uncle Steve say I never travel alone and they're right. I meet new people all the time and enjoy chatting and connecting with all types of people. Despite being bummed about the Red Sox losing to the White Sox twice, I don't remember the smile leaving my face during those games in Fenway Park.

And I had no idea I'd be back in Boston the next summer for a third time and that I'd be driving—instead of flying—all the way home.

There are so many amazing elements to the epic road trip I took that summer after landing in Boston to drive my neighbor Kerry's car back across the country. (I've left out many details in order to focus on the most important aspects of the trip.) I met some great people, spent quality time with family and friends along the way, and saw beauty in all of the states I passed through. At the end of my solo trip across America, I had a newfound sense of independence and freedom.

More importantly, I had a stronger sense of having replaced the love of one person with the love of many. Naturally, these concepts mean different things to everyone depending where each of us is on our life's journey. For me, the trip happened at the perfect time and provided clarity and understanding of where I had been and where I was headed in life. (Although I still didn't have all the answers—does anybody?— I was fortunate to be on a good path.)

BOSTON TO BOISE SOLO ROAD TRIP HIGHLIGHTS

In Boston, Kerry had arranged for me to spend a couple nights with her longtime friends CJ and Erin. They were amazing hosts and also helped get me to and from the T stations—Boston's subway system. The second night I was in town, one of the best rivalries in baseball played out at Fenway Park: the New York Yankees vs. the Boston Red Sox. The energy was electric in a sold-out Fenway.

Fortunately, I had purchased a Standing Room Only ticket online after Kerry and I started planning my trip at dinner a few days prior. CJ and Erin's retired father, Tom, worked as an usher in the Centerfield Triangle Section of the ballpark, so I made my way out there early in the game. Tom greeted me as if I was a longtime family friend and promptly said he'd saved me a seat in the front row. (Believe me, I appreciate every time great things like this happen.) A long-time season ticket holder Tom knew wasn't using the seat, so I got to sit there that night. I sat next to some friendly and entertaining fans and the Sox beat the Yanks in an exciting game. Needless to say, I enjoyed the experience immensely.

Afterward, Tom took a picture of me in the Red Seat located in right field (Google it; cool baseball history stuff) and took me around parts of the historic ballpark I hadn't seen the previous summer. I ate pizza with Tom and other Fenway employees, and we waved to David "Big Papi" Ortiz—one of the most famous players in recent Red Sox history—as he left Fenway a while after the game ended. (Boston, you are wicked cool and I look forward to the next time I can get back!)

COOPERSTOWN, NEW YORK:
THE MAJOR LEAGUE BASEBALL HALL OF FAME

After dropping by her parent's house (Red and Dottie) the next morning to pick up some things for the trip—and a care package Kerry had thoughtfully asked her mom to give me—I headed for Cooperstown. With the goodies Kerry had ready for me sitting in the passenger seat, I excitedly mapped the directions on my phone and looked forward to visiting the quaint town that is home to the baseball Hall of Fame. Driving across Massachusetts into upstate New York that day was beautiful, and it officially kicked off the solo part of my trip. Cooperstown was a place I wanted to visit for decades, and I'm happy to report I went into the Hall wearing a Dodger cap. (Baseball fans will appreciate this inside joke.)

Walking among the displays and reading plaques about some of the greatest players to ever play baseball gave me goosebumps. Being there was another realization of a boyhood dream, and I found myself getting a little emotional as I read the histories of some of the players and memorabilia that can only be found in the Hall of Fame. Getting caught up in the moment is not a bad thing. Being human is better than not feeling any sort of passion—or compassion—for things we are drawn to in life.

I'm drawn to many things in life, and baseball history brings out that inner compassion for certain players, teams and moments from the past. One of the best things about being at the Hall was talking with other baseball fans with whom I shared a common bond. Connecting people of all ages, socioeconomic backgrounds and locations has always been one of baseball's best qualities. And this, too, is on display every day at the Hall of Fame.

After spending three hours winding my way throughout the Hall, I still wasn't ready to leave. The Hall is such a special place to visit if you're a fan of baseball, especially if you appreciate the history of the game. I could've stayed three more hours and still not felt like I adequately covered everything I wanted to see and read. However, I still needed to eat dinner and find a place to spend the night.

With the goal of trying to be less of a Type A planning person, I decided not to plan in advance where I'd be staying every night on the trip. So after leaving Boston, the events of each day helped determine where I ended up each night. This meant there were several nights ahead of me that were up in the air. I felt this was necessary as I continued evolving into the next phase of my life. It was challenging and fun not having everything mapped out beforehand. Everyone knows life isn't mapped out either and requires constant adjustments. So feeling free to decide where I wanted to stay along my road trip—rather than limiting myself to where I needed to be at all times—was liberating, challenging and fun. (Give it a try if you haven't already. For some, it will likely be a mind scrambler. For others, you'll be pleasantly surprised where you end up.)

PITTSBURGH, PENNSYLVANIA: PNC PARK

Heading to Pittsburgh the next day was as unique, fun, and unplanned as any day could ever be. When I woke up that morning in a tiny, northern Pennsylvania town—one of only two nights I spent money on a hotel room throughout the entire trip—I didn't know I'd be doing anything other than driving to watch a day game in the Steel City. After passing through Williamsport— where the Little League World Series was being played—I arrived at PNC Park early that afternoon.

As I pulled into the Home Plate Parking Lot, a family of

four handed me their parking permit. I offered to pay them, but they declined and said something had come up and they couldn't stay for the day game. Since they already paid for parking, they wanted me to use their permit. (This has happened at a couple of ballparks around the country and makes me happy to be a baseball fan.) After thanking them, I headed toward the home plate entrance to buy a ticket for the game which was about to start.

While crossing the street, I met a friendly Pittsburgh Pirate fan. He said he was looking to burn some time that afternoon before picking up his grandchildren later that night. And, like me, Bill hadn't purchased a game ticket yet. While he walked down the outside of the ballpark to the ATM, I waited at the front gate. Meanwhile, a fan who was already in the ballpark came up to me and said he had a free ticket and handed it to me through the gate. (I thanked him and laughed while thinking to myself: #winning). I told Bill what happened, and he said with a big smile, "Welcome to Pittsburgh." He then bought a ticket in the all-you-can-eat section located down the right field side of the ballpark and said we'd both be able to enjoy as much ballpark food as we wanted. When I offered to pay him, Bill said my money was no good that day. (Yep, the game was definitely off to a great start.)

I told Bill about my ritual of walking the entire stadium before sitting down to watch the game. He chuckled and said he'd be my shadow and found it enjoyable seeing the ballpark from my "rookie" perspective. (By the way, PNC Park is a gem that easily ranks in the Top 5 ballparks I've visited so far.) My new friend and I settled into our seats after loading up on hot dogs and nachos—must haves, especially when watching a day game—and Bill explained some of the nuances of the ballpark and the city of Pittsburgh.

As a former police officer, he told me stories of chasing and pulling people out of the Allegheny River, which is located a hop and a skip over the right field fence. One of my favorite aspects of the ballpark is that the right field wall stands exactly 21 feet tall as a tribute to legendary right fielder Roberto Clemente. He wore the number for the Pirates and is a distinguished member of the Baseball Hall of Fame. He was one of Bill's favorite players, and although I never saw him play, I've always truly admired Clemente the ballplayer and the person. (I highly suggest you take a break from reading this chapter and look up Clemente and read about his baseball career and the tragic—yet heroic—way his life ended.) Amazing ballplayer and an even better human being.

I enjoyed Bill's company and stories so much that the ballgame became entirely secondary that afternoon. Traveling allows you the opportunity to meet new people and hear perspectives you may not otherwise have the chance to. Bill was an excellent example of this. After the game, Bill asked if I wanted to grab a beer in the Strip District, which is across the Roberto Clemente Bridge and opposite the North Side section where PNC and Heinz Field are located. (Sounded great to me, especially in the more fluid mindset I was continuing to embrace.) We both hopped in our cars, and I thought we'd be sitting in a line of post-game vehicles, but instead went on a car chase that Bill was accustomed to and I was not.

Bill knew a shortcut to beat the traffic after the game, but said I'd have to drive aggressively and stay on his tail. About 20 minutes later—after frantically driving the streets and alleys of Pittsburgh like I was the one trying to apprehend someone—we made it to a pub. It was a place where Pirates, Steelers and Penguins fans have been celebrating—and drowning their sorrows—for years. And it was a great place to catch my breath, too, after the exhilarating car chase I had successfully completed. Bill knew the streets so well and exposed how much of a newbie I was to the Steel City. (I couldn't repeat the route we took even if you'd asked me five minutes after doing so.) It was a fun and thrilling car chase, but I'm lucky I didn't hit a dumpster, a building or another car. During our pint, we both got a good laugh at how it all might've looked if we'd had a camera crew with us.

Then we walked down the block to another local tavern owned by a buddy of Bill's. The owner treated me like an old friend, and Bill told me more entertaining stories from his days as a police officer in the Burgh. In both pubs, people from all backgrounds came in and said hi and shook Bill's hand while chatting and laughing with us. It felt like I knew these people and was a longtime resident of the city too. The camaraderie that comes from making authentic connections with other human beings is one of the most powerful feelings I experience when traveling. You can search for these types of connections, or they can find you. Either way, soak them up because there's an energy that exists in some connections with random people that isn't easily replicated in our everyday interactions with people we know.

Bill and I thanked his friend and the people we'd been chatting and laughing with as we left the pub to visit a famous market and sandwich shop—Primanti Brothers—a few blocks down the street. The friendly owner offered me anything I wanted to eat, free of charge. (Again, making me feel like an old resident of the city returning to the neighborhood.) I politely declined since I was stuffed from all the food Bill and I consumed at the game. The owner walked me around the historical establishment while showing me framed black and white pictures and telling me the history of his family owning the place for decades. I enjoyed all of it, and when Bill asked if I wanted to go check out another section of the city, I reminded him that a drive to Cleveland was still ahead of me that night. Neither of us wanted the day to end, but we both laughed and hugged and exchanged phone numbers since we knew I had to get back on the road. Bill and I have remained connected ever since that awesome day.

Several days later—as I was leaving Kansas and driving up to Denver—I listened to a voicemail on my phone. It was from an officer saying there was a helicopter tracking me and a roadblock at the Colorado border waiting to end my trip. Since it was morning and I was tired, it took me a moment to recognize the voice. I called Bill immediately and we laughed like old pals. Meeting great people along the journey happens often whenever I travel, and it's one of my favorite things about being able to get away. (I love where I live, so coming home after being on the road and in the air isn't bad either.) On that solo road trip, I met so many kind people and experienced how much *good* there is in the world. Throughout my life, I've learned when you treat people with kindness and respect, you'll often get back double what you give to others.

CLEVELAND, OHIO: PROGRESSIVE PARK (FORMERLY JACOBS FIELD)

Somewhere along the way I contacted Kyle, my good friend in Portland, and told him about my epic adventure. His parents and siblings live outside Cleveland, and I suggested they join me for a ballgame. They are wonderful people and offered me a place to stay for the night after hearing about my trip. I'd planned on staying in a hotel after leaving Pittsburgh, but getting to spend time with Kyle's parents and siblings was even better. Their hospitality was so generous and greatly appreciated.

The next morning, we went to Lake Erie, so I could say I'd seen another one of the Great Lakes. (Lake Superior and Lake Michigan being the other two I'd visited on my travels with Brooke.) Before the game that night, we took pictures outside the Rock & Roll Hall of Fame and ate a delicious and filling pre-game meal at Panini's Gateway Bar & Grill. (Try their amazing sandwiches stuffed with coleslaw and fries. You won't need to eat the rest of the day.) Kyle's four youngest siblings drove us downtown, and we all watched the Los Angeles Angels-Cleveland Indians game at Progressive Field. Kyle's sister, Olivia, even got an autographed ball from one of the players in the bullpen (another example of how fleeting connections can still be meaningful). We all had such a good time together, and I'm fortunate they were willing to go to the game with me that night.

After the post-game fireworks, Indians manager Terry Francona zipped by us on his scooter as we made our way to the parking garage and he made his way home. Would've been fun to meet him, but it didn't happen. While Kyle and Shelea couldn't fly out from Portland to be there that time, the three of us have created so many fun memories over the years since I got divorced. We have developed a special friendship over the past decade that I truly cherish.

Two months after we attended that game, the Cleveland Indians were battling the Chicago Cubs in the World Series. Kyle's mom and brother attended Game 1 of the World Series—held in Cleveland—and Connor caught a foul ball and texted me a picture as I watched the game live on TV. I was excited for them attending Game 1 of the World Series—something I'd love to do—and for him catching a prized foul ball as well. I feel like catching a ball and attending a World Series game will happen for me one of these days, too. (Convenient baseball metaphor: while I'm surrounded by many people I love, I have yet to catch the love of my life.)

ILLINOIS: THE QUAD CITIES

As I landed in Boston to start my road trip, my friend Brooke texted me for the first time in a year or so and asked what I'd

119

been doing all summer. After letting her know about the funny timing of her text, I explained I'd be spending a couple days in Boston before driving west across the country. She mentioned she'd be visiting her family in Illinois a few days from then, which was about the same time I'd be driving across the state. When she invited me to spend a night at her mom's house, I decided to take them up on the offer. Again, it's not lost on me how fortunate I am for these well-timed opportunities—especially on that amazing journey.

After the game in Cleveland, I drove west and spent my only other night in a hotel room on the trip. As I made my way through Ohio and Indiana and into Illinois the next day, I thought about the various people and moments which had positively impacted my life, particularly since my divorce. Brooke was one of the people who had a major impact on me, and I was looking forward to catching up with her and her mom that night. We hadn't communicated for a while, and it was great to talk about all the places we had traveled beginning a year or so after I got divorced.

In Illinois, we enjoyed a moonlit soak in a hot tub overlooking a nearby pond as we laughed and talked about life and the different paths we all take along our individual journeys. The conversation was as relaxing as the warm water on my road-weary muscles. I appreciated all of the wonderful travel opportunities Brooke had helped make possible a year after the divorce and thanked her again during our time together that night. Spending time with Brooke and her mom made me grateful for the incredible timing and circumstances of her contacting me again. I wasn't sure when we'd see each other again, and that night was another example of things happening right on time. Since then, our lives have gone in separate directions, and although we aren't in constant contact, our friendship that began so many years ago is still intact.

A few years prior, I was fortunate to spend time with her family at a time when I no longer attended similar events with an entire family of in-laws to which I belonged for so many years. My former in-laws always treated me well throughout all the years I was married. Time with Brooke's family felt like being with my former in-laws and also provided inspiration to continue seeking new experiences. I didn't take anything for granted and was enjoying the road trip immensely with each passing day driving west.

KANSAS: FAMILY ROOTS

Throughout the adventure across the country, I passed time listening to music, thinking about all kinds of topics, and reflecting on my journeys—including the current road trip—and the bigger "road trip" of my life. For me, road trips have always been about the sights, sounds and time to think along the way—not just the destination at the end of each day. I allow my mind to wander from topic to topic, and although I naturally spend more time on some topics than others, my wonderful family comes up whenever I travel. I've spent considerable time thinking about my immediate family members and how our relationships have changed—both positively and negatively—over the years. (I think about my extended family, too, of course, but I'm obviously much closer to my siblings, so that's my focus here. Big hugs to everyone.)

As families change by expanding and contracting during the passage of time, naturally there are shifts in relationship dynamics. As much change as we've had in our family, we still remain relatively close, and for that I'm grateful. Of course, I'd love to say we're all as close as when we were younger, but that's both an idealistic and unrealistic standard to hold most families to. I know there are some families that have somehow made it happen—to a certain extent—but all family dynamics go through ups and downs and change over time. Each of my five siblings has families of their own—I'm the lone exception—and that naturally leads to a shift in priorities, responsibilities and the amount of time we all spend together. Overall, I feel so fortunate to have a loving mom and stepdad, thoughtful siblings and amazing nieces and nephews. I'm always grateful whenever we're able to spend time with each other individually and as a group. And that will never change.

Driving through Nebraska and Kansas also brought family to mind, especially since my mom was born in Kansas and much of the family on her side still lives in those two states. My mom contacted her Aunt Vonna and Uncle Larry who lived in western Kansas to see if they would be home when I drove through the state, and fortunately they were. They graciously offered me a comfortable place to spend the night before I made my way up to Denver for the final ballpark and game I'd be seeing on the trip. When I arrived in Kansas that evening, the three of us sat around the kitchen table enjoying a cold Pepsi and a big slice of apple pie—perfect for the Americana-themed road trip I was on—and we talked and laughed well past midnight. It was the kind of night and conversation I cherished long after I left their Kansas farm.

Uncle Larry and Aunt Vonna described my mom as a young girl and shared stories of my aunts and uncles as kids before they moved to Idaho when Mom was a teen. The conversation made me appreciate my roots, which were partially sown in the Kansas soil my mom was raised on. Getting to spend more time talking with Aunt Vonna and Uncle Larry the next day was special. As we drove around the farm, they explained the history of their property, which they'd farmed for decades. Hearing their stories about when my mom and my grandfather lived in Kansas made me wistful as I imagined how life must've been long before I was born.

Hearing the stories from long ago reminded me of my younger days when I wished for a grandpa to talk about baseball and life with. Unfortunately it wasn't in the cards. Both of my grandpas died before I was 10 years old. Sadly, Uncle Larry passed away less than two years after my visit to Kansas, so it was the last time I talked to him and enjoyed his warm personality and great sense of humor. As with the passing of my dad and other family and friends over the years, death reminds us all to cherish the moments and times we spend alone and together. (After all, we never know when the last time will be the last time with anyone.)

DENVER, COLORADO: COORS FIELD

Before leaving their farm the next day, I hugged Uncle Larry and Aunt Vonna and made my way toward the Rocky Mountains for the final ballpark on my very memorable—for many reasons that went beyond baseball—road trip that began in Boston. As I was making my way across the country, Kerry had arranged for me to spend a night with some friends of hers when I arrived in Denver. Christine and Heather were gracious hosts, and although we didn't get to spend much time together, they did give me a ride to Coors Field and a place to spend the night. Both of them had to be up early for work the next morning, so I went to the final game on my journey alone and Ubered home after the game to a quiet house. After over a week spent on the road visiting numerous cities, sites and people, my trip—and summer—was winding down.

Things worked out well the moment I arrived at Coors Field that night starting with buying a ticket outside the ballpark from a guy selling them for $4. (Yes, four bucks for an MLB game!) The seat was located in the Rock Pile section in deep center field. Since I was going solo and seating is not highly important to me—especially when my focus is on exploring the whole ballpark—I didn't watch a single inning from my seat. Instead, venturing around the park and sitting in several different sections—while taking pictures—provided numerous vantage points from which to watch the game. In the years since the divorce, connecting with people helped pick me up on so many occasions. That entire trip gave me a new type of energy and the feeling of being surrounded by the love of many and not missing the love of one.

The journey also provided various perspectives from the fans I chatted with at each game. That night, we talked about all things baseball and, specifically, the Rockies and their opponent on that weeknight, the Washington Nationals. And I loved all of it. Enjoying a beautiful night for baseball was a perfect way to wrap up the Ballpark Bucket List portion of my adventure. As I stood outside Coors Field after the game, two couples struck up a conversation with me and invited me to join them across the street at a pub for a nightcap. Again, going with the flow and being friendly and flexible provided a fun way to wrap up the night with some interesting and friendly Denver locals.

HEADING FOR HOME: FREE AT LAST

In the morning I began the next-to-last leg of my journey by driving from Denver to Salt Lake City. My youngest sister Amanda—and my nieces Bella and Brooklyn and nephew Jo— live north of the city and I was looking forward to seeing them and spending the night. Driving across a section of Colorado and Utah I hadn't seen for many years, I thought about the amazing places and people I was fortunate to see and spend time with on this journey. Listening to Spotify playlists I'd made for the trip, along with my stations on Pandora, provided a legendary road trip soundtrack. (If my book ever gets made into a movie, the music from my Boston to Boise road trip should make up the majority of the movie soundtrack... at least if Hollywood wants to stay true to my story.)

Spending the final night of my trip with my sister and her family added more bookmarks to my mental scrapbook as we squeezed in time for ice cream, playing Uno and sharing our stories about summer. Looking back at pictures from that trip makes me smile and also makes me a little sad at how quickly life flies by, especially when seeing how much my nieces and nephew have changed over the past few years. It also made me reflect on my own post-divorce transition from being lonely and depressed to feeling increasingly independent and *happier* throughout that cross-country journey.

Some unexpected travel experiences within the first year after divorce helped take some of the sting out of the divorcee blues. But the Boston to Boise road trip a couple years later was the culmination of all the things I'd learned during the various transitional phases I traveled through after divorcing. Instead of focusing on the next town I'd need to stop for food, gas and lodging on that trip, I began seeing the bigger picture of how many people and places were yet to be encountered— and appreciated—along my journey. Put another way, I was subconsciously seeking to replace the love I once had for one person with the love I was giving and receiving from friends— old and new—and while reconnecting with family.

SOMETIMES YOU FIND YOURSELF IN THE MIDDLE OF NOWHERE

There were two times I found myself getting lost on my epic

road trip. One time was quite accidental in Northern Pennsylvania. The other time—in the middle of Kansas—was intentional. After leaving Cooperstown and the Baseball Hall of Fame earlier on the trip, I used Google Maps and headed west—unsure where I'd spend the night. When I started feeling sleepy, I pulled over and searched for "motels nearby" and within a half hour I was out in the middle of the countryside somewhere north of Williamsport, Pennsylvania. (As we all know, Google Maps isn't always accurate.) It wasn't yet midnight on a cloudless and dark night. All the stars were out, so I took a moment to get out of the car and stare up at the beautiful night sky.

Instead of worrying or being afraid, I took some deep breaths of the sweet summer air and started looking for familiar constellations. A sensation of contentment came over me although I was completely alone in a place I'd never been, but somehow felt absolutely at peace. After a short time of stargazing, I navigated to a nearby town to spend the night. (I slept for five hours before getting up early and driving to Pittsburgh for an incredible day with my new friend Bill.) Moments like staring up at the night sky alone in the middle of nowhere in Pennsylvania stick with me because they are memorable, liberating and good for the soul. In quiet moments like that—standing completely alone and unafraid of the unknowns ahead—feeling the vastness of life and the love of family and friends is incredibly powerful.

Before getting to my aunt and uncle's farm several days later, I stopped in the early evening to take a picture at a crossroad out in the middle of endless Kansas farmland. Pulling off the main highway and driving a few miles, I parked next to a vast field and hung out for several minutes while snapping a few pictures of the beautiful land and sky surrounding me. The trip provided the opportunity to enjoy the freedom that comes from isolation.

For years I'd been married to one person and came to define myself by our marriage. During these times of solitude on the road—of which there were many—I realized this trip was a big step toward self-discovery. At a time when I was at a crossroads in life, I was reintroducing myself to who I used to be, who I was and who I was becoming. Although I'd interacted with lots of people in Boston and along the entire journey, realizing how happy I could be even when completely alone was monumental.

REPLACING ONE WITH MANY

A couple of years before taking my cathartic and liberating solo road trip across the country, I was over my ex-wife. While driving from Boston to Boise at the end of the summer, I felt more independence and freedom than at any other point in my life. This served as a reminder that it was possible to continue feeling this way going forward. There was confidence and power which flowed from this overdue realization.

Equally important, I realized although the married version of me hadn't been a good fit for my former wife, it didn't mean the current—and future—version of me would be a bad fit for any woman I'd eventually meet. Nobody is perfect. It was vital to my growth process to understand I didn't need some drastic overhaul to become someone else when who I was, who I am and who I will be is more than good enough. These realizations were a giant leap forward in my personal growth and evolution toward directing my future. While my unwritten chapters were not solely mine to direct—since other factors are constantly present to influence our decisions in life—I began to see more fully the possibilities my future chapters could have.

For some people, it's a natural reaction to withdraw after a breakup or divorce. I went the opposite direction. Initially, my friendly nature took a hit, and I withdrew from friends and family at times, but decided to start putting myself out there after being divorced for several months. Being flexible and approachable allowed me to connect with many people I would've never encountered had I remained withdrawn or closed off to others. All of us go through a growth process on various levels throughout our lives. The only difference is when and on which levels we are impacted. I used to feel like my process took much longer—and started later—than it should have. However, I began understanding the truth of being where we are at any given moment is a process. And this process directs us to our present and future moments so that we might understand more fully the *why* and *how* we arrive at a place at any given point along our journey.

I continued reminding myself that although it seemed late to me, the process was actually right on time. (My friends and family may read this section and wonder why I'm not on time more often in the chronological sense. But now isn't the time for that conversation. Yes, pun intended.) During the married chapter of my life, things became stagnant and I became complacent. Life immediately following the divorce—and especially on my solo adventure across the country—gave my Single Guy phase a happy jolt which opened the door to my New Man phase. Naturally, these phases and chapters are different for everyone.

My married life had been primarily built around one person, but was being replaced by connecting with so many people who provided a new level of balance in my life. Throughout my travels, I realized my present and future were being built around the many people already in my life—and the many more I'd met since divorcing. New doors had opened, and other unforeseen doors would potentially offer even more opportunities. I appreciated the idea that my path to true independence and happiness was being paved before me, and I liked the direction it was heading.

"See the world. Meet new people. Find yourself.
Have a story worth telling."

– Anonymous

LONDON AND PARIS:

Perspective

JOURNAL ENTRY (CIRCA 2019)

When the calendar turns and a new year begins, I like reflecting on the previous year. I think back on goals accomplished, places I traveled and whether or not I achieved any meaningful growth. During the early summer of 2018, I flew to Washington, D.C. to spend five days with my Great-Aunt Lena and Great-Uncle Gary. I was excited about my first trip to our nation's capital because I'd always wanted to see the Capitol, the White House and the Washington and Lincoln Memorials, among others.

Gary took me on his infamous "Death March of the Monuments," and although that was a hot and humid day, I loved it all. Getting to stand where Martin Luther King Jr. gave his famous "I Have a Dream Speech" in 1963 was powerful and moving. Being there allowed me to see this iconic place differently and imagine what it must've felt like being in the crowd that day. Visiting so many museums that week fed my history-loving appetite and I still want to go back for more. Of course, checking off two more stadiums from my Ballpark Bucket List by attending an Orioles-Nationals game at Nationals Park and a Marlins-Orioles game at Camden Yards didn't hurt either. Camden Yards is now on my Top 5 Ballparks List. Spending time with Lena and Gary in D.C. was fun and so many memories were made.

I also took a solo drive to Gettysburg National Military Park the first morning after arriving in D.C. I spent that day driving and walking around the beautiful, serene location in Southern Pennsylvania. I felt a sense of awe and sadness at the legendary Civil War battlefield site. At one point, I intentionally got out of the car to sit and lean against one of the makeshift rock walls—only a few feet tall—for a little while. I listened to the sounds of the birds on that warm and sunny June day while looking across a field that once was covered with fallen soldiers. Contrasting the peaceful, rolling green fields with what took place there brought to life the horrors of the battle in a way the famous black and white photos never quite could. The inner historian in me tried to imagine what it must have felt like to be a soldier in the Battle of Gettysburg on that hallowed ground back in 1863.

Gettysburg and the National Monuments of D.C. heightened my sense of awareness of time and place and provided the opportunity to be open to perspectives outside my usual periphery. I love where I live and mostly enjoy the typical days in my typical life. However, I really appreciate being in different locations and situations since it forces my senses and awareness levels to fully engage. And there are times I literally feel the perspective shifts occurring as I move from place to place. If you allow for it, travel can have this type of impact.

And that's when I found myself in London looking up at Parliament and Big Ben while reflecting on how I'd arrived there...

The year and a half between my solo trip from Boston to Boise and a trip to London and Paris in March of 2018 was filled with many more incredible travel adventures. The amount of travel that began less than a year after divorce—and mostly paused during a year of grad school—continued at a steady clip. To wit, a trip to Vancouver, British Columbia a few weeks after returning from my epic cross-country road trip was followed up with another solo visit to the Oregon Coast that fall. On the heels of a flight to Vegas for a fun weekend in February, I took a solo road trip to Portland and the Oregon Coast in March. (Have I mentioned the Oregon Coast is one of my Happy Places? Just checking.)

While on a work trip that June, I enjoyed my second ballgame at beautiful Petco Park in San Diego watching a Braves-Padres game. Then squeezed in a quick weekend in Seattle for a Rays-Mariners game at underrated Safeco Field (now T-Mobile) with my buddy Kyle and his brother Sean. (If you haven't been, I highly recommend you make a trip to that gorgeous Pacific Northwest ballpark.) Spending time with all of the friends I've met post-divorce has been incredibly rewarding and often feels like we've known each other much longer than we actually have.

Reflecting on the amount of travel I've been fortunate to experience in the years since getting divorced always makes me pause to appreciate where I've been—both literally and figuratively. Traveling was my primary therapy in the year or so after divorce, but has become my source of inspiration and happiness in the years since. Many times I've caught myself thinking, "I'm fortunate to be doing this right now." In the several years since divorcing, I've traveled to more places than during my entire marriage. Instead of letting my travels become routine, I've continued to recognize and appreciate my situation more with each passing year.

Scott Looney

SAYING YES TO TRAVEL OPPORTUNITIES

Most of my trips during this time were planned in advance, which is necessary as a teacher on a budget. Like many people, I've always had the mantra of work hard, play hard. (But this requires saving hard too.) Another solo trip to the Oregon Coast in July was followed up with my second trip in as many summers to Austin to visit my cousin Megan, her husband Brian, and their daughter Mckenzie. The four of us took a road trip to Houston for an Angels-Astros game and checked Minute Maid Park off my Ballpark Bucket List. They liked exploring the ballpark's various quirks and vantage points as much as I did, which made my pre-game ritual all the more enjoyable that day. (Joining me on my ballpark walkabout is never a requirement of anyone who is with me, but it's fun seeing the stadium from perspectives other than my own too.) Throughout that weekend, we chatted and laughed as we tried scoring points at Top Golf, played a couple games of Acquire—our favorite board game—and savored more delicious Texas BBQ. I was also happy Manny's younger brother, Miguel, was able to join us at the ballgame. The trip included baseball, golf, great food and drinks and lots of laughs—everything I could ever want in a vacation.

I even met a woman—at a random gas station, of all places—on our drive back from Houston and discovered we attended the same ballgame earlier that day. Meeting her was an unexpected bonus as we wound up having a long-distance relationship for the next six months. When her Astros and my Dodgers met in the World Series that October, we talked up our teams and discussed meeting up at one of the games. We were unable to get tickets to a World Series game and I'm still bitter at the outcome of that 7-game Series. (Baseball fans know what I'm referring to here. If you're not a fan, look up the Astros 2017 World Series scandal and you'll understand my disdain for the outcome.)

Our short time together was very enjoyable, especially since we both are baseball fans and teachers. The opportunity to travel and experience new places in Texas—such as The Alamo in San Antonio after a delicious Thanksgiving dinner with her family—created more good memories. However, the old adage that long-distance relationships rarely last proved to be true, and ours ended amicably in early 2018. (Cue one of my favorite U2 songs: "I Still Haven't Found What I'm Looking For.") Although I was more than ready for a serious relationship at the time, my search for the next special someone continued onward.

The purpose of recounting the trips I planned, saved up for and enjoyed during the time between my epic Boston to Boise road trip and the vacation to London and Paris isn't to boast. Instead, it's to demonstrate my appreciation for the travel opportunities I've continually experienced since becoming a divorcee. If someone had told me a few years earlier that I'd be visiting so many places across America and Europe, I wouldn't have believed it. Sometimes it *still* catches me off guard when reflecting on the sheer amount of traveling I've been able to fit into a relatively short time span in my life.

The stories in this book do not include every road trip or flight since the divorce, but most of the main ones have been covered. The travel experiences I've left out of this book do not diminish how much I enjoyed those trips. (Instead they have been excluded in the interest of keeping you interested in reading the stories which *are* included in this book.) I also remind myself of how much of my travels have been possible based on getting myself off the couch and saying YES more. Making myself available to the incredible number of opportunities which have come my way beginning about six months after becoming a divorcee helped launch me into this new chapter of my life.

I've discussed many of my travel stories with people, and I'm repeatedly asked the same thing: "Do you ever work?" It's a fair question that makes me laugh every time I hear it. The answer, of course, is yes. Since becoming an educator, I've worked harder and consistently put in more hours than for any job I've ever had—and I continue doing so. (Taking my own advice, I continue going on trips when I can, while I can.) Unfortunately, despite trying for several years now, I still don't love the job of teaching. However, all of the thoughtful and amazing students I've been fortunate to know is what keeps me in the profession. I have some very talented colleagues—which I've learned a great deal from—whom I count as friends as well. As a teacher, I do appreciate the earned time off, but more importantly, I value the positive relationships I've built with my students, their parents and my coworkers over the years. These connections sustain me as an educator and have always meant the world to me. And they always will.

SAYING YES TO LIVING LIFE
TO THE FULLEST

Realizing the great travel times were a combination of working hard, planning ahead and getting some lucky breaks along the way (or was it creating my own luck?) made me understand these experiences didn't necessarily have to end. I realized they didn't necessarily get to continue either. This reality helped me appreciate each experience as it unfolded and not to take anything for granted.

Traveling with friends and family provided happiness and renewed a sense of hope for my future chapters. It also provided several experiences around America—and around Europe—I may not otherwise have been able to enjoy. Being divorced allowed time to reconnect with the people I wanted to spend more time with, which marriage hadn't regularly allowed. Making oneself available is also an important attitude and mindset which has continually served me well. By frequently saying yes, I found myself in new situations and meeting new people, which would not have been possible if I'd stayed home and in my comfort zone.

During the cold depths of winter, a friend offered an excellent plan for a vacation to two cities I didn't envision visiting until much later in life. So when the chance for my second journey to Europe arose, I jumped at it. My buddy and I dubbed the weeklong trip to London and Paris that spring "The Tale of Two Cities" trip. We visited some iconic locations in both cities and enjoyed some delicious culinary experiences as well. (I mean, if you don't enjoy the amazing cuisine in Paris, you're not doing it right.) Thinking about how far I'd come—literally and figuratively—in the time since divorce made me pause when standing in front of Parliament and Big Ben. Seeing the buildings and cities I'd only seen on TV and online gave me an opportunity to appreciate how fortunate I was to be standing there at all.

Smiling proudly, I pondered how a guy from a small town in Idaho—just a few years removed from starting completely over and transitioning through the life stages often associated with earlier adulthood—was visiting so many iconic places on the other side of the world. As I'd felt when visiting some cherished ballparks in America, happy tears welled up in my eyes while taking in the scenery on that trip to London and Paris. Plans for visiting many of these places occupied space in my mental agenda for *someday*, but making someday into *today* made me realize how fortunate I was to be doing so. Reflecting on how much growth I'd experienced—and how much my life had changed—as I looked at the famous structures gave me a strange sense of accomplishment. By continually reflecting on where we've been, we honor the challenges and effort it takes to make our present experiences a reality—and our future experiences as well.

"MIND THE GAP!"

Being a new teacher meant bringing work along while on Spring Break in London and Paris. I resent spending time working during any vacation. I've always felt vacations are earned and, therefore, time shouldn't have to be used doing anything work-related. Unfortunately, it's rare to be able to totally unplug—from either work or technology—in the times in which we live. Some people are fine with working while on vacation, but I'm not a member of that group. (To the best of my knowledge, nobody ever says on their deathbed they wish they'd worked more.) However, I didn't mind spending a couple hours upstairs in an eatery located right next to the newest version of the Globe Theatre in London. After all, there are worse places to spend an afternoon than overlooking the River Thames and enjoying a pint of Guinness with lunch—a tip o' the cap to my Irish roots—whilst working from a laptop. (Having ol' Bill Shakespeare's plays performed next door added a welcome dose of inspiration as well.)

We walked a lot and rode The Tube—where I heard the infamous "Mind the gap!" for the first time—on our travels around London. It took riding The Tube and continually hearing "Mind the gap!" for me to understand what Londoners have long known about the danger of entering and exiting the subway cars. Taking in all the tourist must-sees like London

Bridge, Parliament and Big Ben among several other places was truly memorable. In jolly old London, Parliament and Buckingham Palace were among my favorite places to visit. The history and architecture in the old town was truly a sight to behold. Strolling the streets, I remember wondering if life would bring me back to this historic city. (I hope so, but who knows what life has in store for any of us?) Taking time to pause for a moment and appreciate the time and space in which I'm living always makes me feel more alive. Traveling provides new perspectives while also keeping things in perspective.

Iconic places are great, but the meals, people and stories which are generated while traveling are often better than the locations I've been intent on seeing. During our time in London, my favorite meal was at a Michelin-rated Indian food restaurant named Gymkhana not far from Hyde Park. (I had to Google Michelin ratings, so if you're like me and are unaware of what being rated means for a restaurant, you should look it up. Go ahead... I'll wait.) Each course was prepared in such a way that it was more than a meal—it was an experience. The presentation, the textures and the flavors were all incredible. And it was worth every bit of the amount paid. Enjoying each course during one of the most delicious meals I've ever eaten was an opportunity I look forward to having again—hopefully with a special someone next time. Meals and moments like this make vacations a bit more memorable than they might otherwise have been.

During the Tale of Two Cities trip, plenty of entertainment was provided while people watching and chatting up Londoners and Parisians whenever the opportunity presented itself. I intentionally made conversation with as many people as possible—something I enjoy doing frequently—at all the places we ate or grabbed a beverage. Chatting with the Uber and taxi drivers along the way was fun as always too. I find most people fascinating, and everyone has a unique story.

Whether traveling domestically or abroad, the vast majority of people I've spent time talking with have been good, friendly humans. Of course, there exists a small number of people I'm glad to have only shared a few minutes of time with. (We've all had these experiences, whether on vacation or otherwise. And they make us value our time talking with the good humans of planet Earth even more.) Overall, most people I've chatted with on my travels have reaffirmed my faith in humanity.

Speaking the same language as everyone else in any country I'm visiting isn't necessary. I've found all that's required is being a decent human being because most people you encounter are decent human beings. Popular and social media often perpetuate stereotypes which are exaggerated and rarely—if ever—true. Traveling abroad opened my eyes and added to my perspective by forcing me to see there's a whole world out there to pursue. So explore and experience different cultures whenever you get the opportunity.

"WE'LL ALWAYS HAVE PARIS"

After taking a train through The Chunnel from England to France—a new experience I was nervous about embarking on—we arrived in Paris. The train ride from London to Paris took a little more than two hours. After rising from the depths of the English Channel and seeing the peaceful French countryside from my window seat while zipping along the tracks, I purposefully took everything in around me. To some passengers, it probably wasn't overly memorable, but I breathed a sigh of relief and gratitude knowing I was fortunate to be riding that train—and also the train of life each of us is riding. We all get one life to live on this planet and at a particular time and place in history. Making the most of it—and living our best life—has become cliché, but why *shouldn't* we make the most of the opportunity? (After all, it's probably not much fun living your *worst* life, right?)

When traveling anywhere—but especially someplace new—I often become hyper-aware of my surroundings. Sights, sounds and smells are heightened. I sometimes try to imagine a place as it might have appeared a decade or many decades ago. This keeps me keenly aware of the present space I'm in—both physically and emotionally—and helps me mentally bookmark places so I can remember how I feel at those particular moments. Since my teenage years, it's something I've done almost subconsciously. Like how I imagine having a photographic memory would be, but with the emotions attached to a picture—not just the image itself.

For me, mental bookmarking is similar to how hearing certain songs takes us back to specific times—and places—in our lives when we can remember *exactly* how we felt at a particular moment. Mental bookmarking doesn't require music, but a song makes attaching emotional memories to moments a little easier. As a result, I truly cherish the number of memories stored in my mental scrapbook over the years. (Regrettably, my short-term memory isn't as good as my long-term. And getting older isn't helping.) I try to add to my mental scrapbook as often as possible because having so many wonderful moments is the "stuff" of life. Material things are nice, but great memories have always been more meaningful to me.

TRAVELING CREATES MEMORIES

I distinctly remember mentally bookmarking as many things as possible while visiting some iconic places in Paris like the Eiffel Tower, the Arc de Triomphe and the Palace of Versailles.

Located outside of Paris, The Palace of Versailles is the site of so many historic moments in French and world history—the Treaty of Versailles was signed in the Hall of Mirrors to officially end World War I over one hundred years ago—and it was even more beautiful than I imagined. Standing inside the Palace—especially in the spacious Hall of Mirrors—was incredible. Having studied and taught about the people and events that have taken place there over the centuries, I could feel the past while soaking in the astonishing beauty of the present.

Another place this happened was while approaching the Notre Dame Cathedral for the first time—around midnight and absent the typical crowds—on the first night in Paris. It was stunningly beautiful at night and having only a few bystanders around felt like we happened upon a rare moment when the hallowed ground was left alone. The next day, after visiting a famous nearby bookstore—named Shakespeare & Company (but ironically located in Paris)—I got a full look at the historic, gothic cathedral which had been visited by untold numbers of people over the centuries.

Standing there on a sunny spring day and seeing the architectural elements up close, I felt a shared sense of awe, much like those who had stood there before me and will stand there long after me. However, it struck me how different seeing the Notre Dame Cathedral at night and then during the day had been. The bustling crowds of daytime—contrasted with the serenity of the cathedral at night—provided insight into how our perspectives can be influenced by the places and times in which we live.

I find that seeking perspective goes hand in hand with connecting to others, whether it's physically, mentally or historically. (Obviously, I'm preachin' to the choir... yes, this pun placement is holy... um, I mean wholly, intended.) At a few locations, I remember closing my eyes and breathing in deeply while exhaling appreciation for all the things I was experiencing. Similar to the green cathedrals I've visited around the United States—where parishioners practice another form of worshiping—the connection to history is palpable. And at that moment—and several others while in London and Paris—I was totally aware of the special time and place in which I was living. Being present is essential to experiencing people, places and events more fully. This gives us the chance to momentarily pause our present so we can appreciate these mental bookmarks as time ceaselessly marches forward.

During the long flights across the Atlantic Ocean, I reflected on my life, especially the recent years while experiencing so many changes. Navigating the tough times along the way helped prove to myself I could get through them—and be better off for doing so. I also reflected on the many people who have been in my corner and helped me along the various paths I've taken—before and after the divorce. All of us should take time to reflect and acknowledge the people, places and moments which have helped us along our journeys. Regularly doing so makes the destinations we eventually reach all the more satisfying.

Traveling opens up opportunities to experience new perspectives, challenges ones we have long held and helps shape new ones as we move forward along our various paths in life. While continuing to transition through the New Man phase, I became less reliant on others in determining my happiness level. Instead, I realized happiness could—and should—be found alone if we are to be truly happy in the presence of others. Being happy with who we are as individuals is essential to being more independent and, therefore, less *dependent* on those around us.

It's the primary reason I've made a point of traveling solo so often in the years after divorcing. Doing so has helped me become more independent but also provided a sense of freedom I didn't realize I *needed*. Looking back from the perspective of time—and distance—allowed for clarity and seeing how my marriage wasn't as great as I'd previously thought. Truly enjoying and finding satisfaction doing things on my own boosted my confidence and helped me get over the *need* to be with someone in order to be happy on a daily basis.

FINDING YOUR BEACH...
OR MOUNTAIN TOP...OR WHATEVER...

One memorable experience to illustrate this point came at the end of that summer—five months upon returning home from the London and Paris trip—and after a couple days hiking and driving solo throughout beautiful Glacier National Park in Montana. During my last night there, I stood alone in the dark at the highest point in the park. Feeling like I was at the top of the world, my eyes took in the vast, star-filled night sky above. Letting my mind wander while pondering how fortunate I was for all of the experiences—solo and otherwise—which literally brought me to that moment made me a little emotional.

I stood there completely alone and smiled at my good fortune while surrounded by nature. Tears streamed freely down my face, loving the idea of how satisfied I had become as a single man who had literally reached the mountain top and experienced true happiness alone. More importantly—especially in that moment of clarity—I envisioned more happiness ahead. My headlights showed I was the only car driving down the Going to the Sun Road late on that Saturday night. Despite being alone, I felt surrounded by the love of family and friends who had helped me arrive at that moment. And the emotions I felt were those of gratitude and appreciation—not fear or loneliness. I had reached another pinnacle of growth.

Alone time can be a positive experience for everyone, especially those people who don't prefer traveling. Some people may not want—or even need—to travel in order to move on from a breakup, divorce or other major life transitions. It's important to find your happy places—whether it's an actual physical space or a mental or emotional space—and to visit as often as you can. We all need to recharge and process where we've been and where we are going. By finding and spending time in the places and spaces that make us happy, we begin to find more beaches and mountain tops in our lives where we feel happiness. (The not-so-hidden metaphor here is my way of saying I hope finding your own happy places will be an enjoyable process.)

For those of you still reeling from divorce or experiencing a difficult breakup, you already know things will be rough at times. But also know you'll likely find yourself better off—on many levels—as time marches on. (I didn't believe this at first, but if you've read this far then hopefully you see there are great things potentially ahead for each of us.) You'll likely realize some negative things about your previous relationship that weren't going to change no matter how long you were together with that person. Over time, I realized how my negativity toward my marriage ending had transitioned into seeing things more objectively and accurately. Time passing after divorce brought me perspective on the past—opening up the present and the future. Without perspective, you might not be fully in the present moment you're now experiencing.

FINDING PERSPECTIVE

Above all, travel can provide perspective on our careers, relationships and life. It doesn't matter if it's around the state, around the country or around the world. When we travel, we can't help but broaden our horizons and expand all of our perspectives. You encounter many different people when traveling, and some people naturally have more of an impact on you than others. You get to see people through a different lens than you would while filling up the gas tank on your way home from work. Because we typically aren't in "work mode" when we travel, we are often more aware of our surroundings, especially when visiting new places.

Traveling to London and Paris that spring helped get me outside my comfort zone and provided a needed shift in perspective. That trip helped me appreciate where I've been but also helped me see where I was going. My love of travel and connecting with people wherever I go is something I thrive on and truly enjoy. Allow yourself to look beyond your own borders—whether it's your relationships, where you work and live or where you want to go—and then get out and live. Hopefully you'll be excited to see what develops. Before long, you'll look back and see things in your life from different angles you might not anticipate. Growth can be an emotional journey, but it's an important and necessary step toward writing our next chapters and moving forward positively.

> *"How far you go in life depends on your being tender with the young, compassionate with the aged, sympathetic with the striving, and tolerant of the weak and strong. Because someday in your life you will have been all of these."*
>
> *– George Washington Carver*

TRAVELING THERE AND BACK AGAIN

JOURNAL ENTRY (CIRCA 2021)

A couple summers ago, my good friend Keisha and I were in Seattle enjoying a Mariners game and taking in the sights and sounds of one of my favorite cities in America. While walking around downtown, we noticed a bar called Bad Bishop, so we dropped in for a cocktail. A handful of people were around the bar, and a few couples sat at the tables in the relatively small, chic bar. After getting our drinks, we decided to have some fun by creating fictional stories and conversations for each person in the place. Visually working our way around the room, we came up with histories and entertaining dialogue for each person. We laughed so much at our spontaneous game that it probably looked like we'd had more than one drink.

Out of curiosity, I looked up the meaning of bad bishop a couple of days after returning home. A bad bishop is a chess reference referring to a bishop being blocked by its own pawns, effectively rendering it temporarily useless. Being with Keisha in Seattle—especially at that time in my life—made me feel *unimpeded* by some of the things in life that had previously been making me feel like the bad bishop in a game of chess.

During the ballgame and while eating dinner afterward in a restaurant downtown, Keisha and I discussed job stresses, empathy fatigue and questioning career choices—all of which were weighing on me at the time. She talked me through some of the challenges I was processing, and her calm, experienced way of offering meaningful suggestions helped tremendously. By talking through why I'd been feeling mentally stuck recently, she offered a fresh perspective, which opened up a new way of thinking. Keisha encouraged me to continually seek and do the things that make me happy despite the obstacles we all face. Her advice was straightforward and practical, and I remind myself of that conversation whenever my focus fades away from doing things that make me happy.

Looking back on the years since divorce, I was grateful to be where I was at that time. Outside of my work stress, my life was going amazingly well. There's no such thing as a perfect life, but I feel happiest when spending time with family and friends and traveling—whether solo or with others. Visiting all of the incredible places I was fortunate to see while meeting so many remarkable people was the part of my life I had no complaints about. Keisha helped me feel less worried about the future unknowns regarding my career, relationships and life. This freed me up to focus more on pursuing happiness along the way.

And that's when I found myself going on more adventures with friends and family—and alone— while continuing to travel along my life's journey...

One awesome aspect of traveling as an independent person is the freedom to travel alone or with family and friends. The choices allow for flexibility in taking certain types of trips that I'd rather not take alone. Traveling overseas by myself isn't overly appealing. So when a friend with plenty of experience traveling abroad asked if I wanted to visit The Netherlands and Germany, it was easy to say yes.

TRAVELING ACROSS THE POND PART 2: AMSTERDAM, NETHERLANDS AND KOBLENZ, GERMANY

Amsterdam offered a glimpse into one of the world's cleanest, greenest and most progressive cities. It typically ranks among the top cities in Europe for air quality, and bicyclists are everywhere. Amsterdam is also a walkable city—and not just in the infamous Red Light District. While strolling through Amsterdam's Red Light District one of the evenings we were in town, I was surprised to be walking amongst so many families—some with children around 10-12 years old. (I'd heard the section has a certain type of beauty both day and night, so I *had* to find out for myself—for research purposes, of course.)

Just like these families, I walked through the famous District as a tourist and gained a new perspective on how this section of Amsterdam lacked the seedy, sketchy appearance I expected it to have. There were pubs and plenty of window shopping to be had, but there were also eateries, ice cream shops and bakeries open late. Speaking with some locals, they explained that while the District's reputation was sketchy for many decades, it had been cleaned up in the past 10-20 years in order to attract more tourists.

Amsterdam is so beautiful and peaceful. The people I chatted with—and there were many, of course—were very friendly, and the relaxed vibe of the city was palpable. And despite the record-high temperatures for each successive day we were there, it was a wonderful place to vacation while experiencing a different culture and seeing some places I hope to visit again.

Many of the aspects I enjoyed most about that trip were discovered along the way to the must-see places on my list. (I've found this is true whether traveling near or far.) Visiting the Vincent Van Gogh museum and Anne Frank's house were high on my list during that trip to Europe. And I highly recommend these places to anyone planning a trip to the area. Along the way, many coffeeshops can be found among the historic buildings and beautiful canal walkways in Amsterdam. They are similar to those in the U.S. but with one significant difference: coffeeshops in Amsterdam offer many varieties of cannabis. So not only is Amsterdam a green city because of its friendliness toward the environment, it offers legal consumption of something else green as well.

Initially, I chuckled at how many people sat outside enjoying a beverage while puffing away on a joint. Police officers smiled and nodded politely as they engaged in conversation or walked on by the people in the beautiful Dutch town. The relaxed vibe of the city and its citizens was quite peaceful. And there were many bakeries in Amsterdam offering goodies which could leave a person feeling a little baked as well—especially in the record-setting heat we endured while walking around the city. (Amster-damn it was hot!) The Dutch are known for being straightforward and practical in their speech, and the city is very much in a forward-thinking part of the world as well. While it's not everyone's cup of tea, it doesn't have to be. (I'd offer a "When in Rome" comment here, but that would be so cliché, right?) Having options in life can be a good thing, and the Dutch make a compelling case for relaxing some restrictions—relatively speaking, of course.

After several days in Amsterdam, my buddy and I traveled by train to Germany and enjoyed delicious, traditional German meals and beers with some fun relatives of his. A river cruise on the Rhine River provided photo opportunities of large historical statues, amazing castles and the beautiful German countryside. Capturing more mental bookmarks was special during my third trip—so far—across the pond. And similar to how fortunate I'd felt when visiting Ireland years ago—the country of my father's heritage—traveling around The Netherlands and Germany provided the opportunity to visit the countries of my mother's heritage. Both trips overseas were more meaningful for these reasons. Connecting to our past is a personal and special way to appreciate those who came before us—whether or not we can trace them back to our own family tree.

While traveling domestically and abroad, I've seen so many famous landmarks, and these places have often stirred my imagination and emotions. But the memories that stay with me the longest are the people I have met and the great conversations we've shared. The unplanned, out-of-the way eateries and pubs I've spent an hour—or three—in and the experiences I've had while traipsing through all types of weather along my journeys have provided much more meaningful stories than simply seeing the iconic locations.

Memories of ducking out of the steady downpouring rain one afternoon in Paris—and enjoying French wine and a fresh charcuterie board at a restaurant whose name I can't recall located down a street I'll never remember—will remain with me forever. Mental bookmarks like crowding into a bustling, old London pub across the street from Parliament—while sharing great travel stories with fellow Americans and members of the British government—are fun to revisit. After all, I might see Parliament again, but I may not get to experience the mixture of people and conversations provided in that first visit. Unexpectedly meeting Keisha and her sister in that pub at that particular time led to a special friendship I might not otherwise have. Sharing a small sample of these stories in this book makes me smile because I haven't always had a chance to share them with friends and family when returning home from my travels.

Moments like talking with other passengers from around the world on a Rhine River cruise—and taking a gondola ride over the vineyards in the small German town of Rudesheim after a traditional German lunch—are more memorable than any of the statues seen on that trip. And I have dozens of other amazing experiences and memories from my trips around America and Europe stored among my mental bookmarks that I haven't mentioned in this book. In my travels, I have found the *pursuit* of historic places and iconic landmarks—at all times of day and in every season—brings me more happiness than the actual locations themselves.

FEELING UNIMPEDED

During a six-week period from mid-June to early August—which included The Netherlands and Germany vacation—I enjoyed unprecedented travel opportunities that particular summer and year. Even surpassing the many unexpected adventures I took during the first year after the divorce. I was amazed at how many opportunities came about. If someone had told me in the early post-divorce period of my life that I'd be traveling this much, I would have laughed until I cried—and the tears would've been from the sadness of feeling like traveling was not within my grasp. It took getting divorced for me to learn what truly makes me happy—and helped me realize how my marriage was impeding the things that made me happiest.

Again, showing and feeling gratitude while marveling at how much I was able to do in such a short time-span helped me appreciate the moments as I experienced them. (Who knows if I'll ever fit that amount of travel into such a relatively short amount of time again?) The things that make each of us happy are out there for all of us to seek and find. We have to look for opportunities—and be open to saying yes—in order for them to happen.

Kicking off that incredible six-week period of travel in early June, the Oregon Coast beckoned me back to the waves to reset my inner clock. From the ocean shores, I drove up to Seattle to meet up with a great friend while watching a Royals-Mariners game on a perfect summer night under the stars. This was followed by driving solo to my family reunion the next day in Eastern Oregon—cherishing time with my family and our annual summer tradition. Being with my mom, step-dad, siblings and amazing nieces and nephews is one aspect of life that makes me happiest— whether at our reunion or our sporadic meetups during any given year.

A little over a week later, I was flying to San Diego for an amazing 4th of July weekend. While in SoCal, traveling by boat for an afternoon on Catalina Island with my friend Keisha was a new and awesome experience for me. We cruised around the island in a golf cart before enjoying a meal overlooking the ocean on that perfectly sunny afternoon. (A guy could get used to that lifestyle.) After a couple days back in San Diego, we took a road trip north to Los Angeles for a beautiful summer afternoon Padres-Dodgers game—my fifth game at Dodger Stadium and Keisha's first—and then visited the famous Griffith Observatory on a gorgeous summer night. The views of the city were incredible and felt like a scene from a movie. (Note to Hollywood execs: I'm open to discussing a movie deal next time I'm in L.A. Let's do lunch.) I loved being back in SoCal and have always found it relaxing. I flew home to Boise the next afternoon with a fresh batch of wonderful memories.

Much of my travel that summer was planned, but some was not. Either way, I was surprised with all of the places I was able to go. (Even Dr. Seuss would've been impressed.) One of the handful of pre-planned trips took shape when my buddy Michael invited me to join him for a couple days while he was in St. Louis attending an economics conference in July. Earlier that spring, he'd mentioned going to a baseball game together. (You already know where this is going.) So a few days after getting home from spending time with Keisha in Southern California, I was on a plane headed to St. Louis to meet up with my longtime friend.

Michael and I watched a Diamondbacks-Cardinals game that night at gorgeous Busch Stadium while surrounded by the wonderful hospitality from people in that great baseball town. The next day, we visited the famous Gateway Arch and ate lunch at the top of the tallest building in the city. A quick, but fun, two days. (Spending a week in one location is great at times, but not entirely necessary in order for me to enjoy traveling.) When Michael flew home later that afternoon, I rented a car and drove solo on I-70 across the state of Missouri. Though it was hot and humid, the road trip within the weekend provided time to reflect on the summer—and life in general. I felt truly fortunate to be going on this remarkable ride, especially considering how far I'd come since divorce—both mentally and physically.

All the travel I was able to do throughout that magical summer of 2019—the last "normal" summer before Covid-19—was incredibly meaningful on many levels. Traveling adventures with friends and family provide some of the best mental bookmarks. I find that recalling the stories from these experiences often provides more laughter and love than the experiences themselves.

When I arrived in Kansas City that night, my cousin Russ and his fiancé Christi greeted me warmly as we laughed about how our plan had come together. At the end of May, when they visited—along with some of our Kansas and D.C. family—some of our Idaho family, I'd told them about my upcoming trip to St. Louis. So the idea of driving across Missouri had been hatched then, which was about a month or so before I flew to

St. Louis. While in Kansas City, I spent a couple of nights with my cousin Angela and her husband Rod, Aunt Vonna—who happened to be visiting from Kansas—and their family. We played cards and laughed late into the night on both occasions, and I remember having sore abs from laughing so much with family.

We even managed to get a little sleep before attending a Tigers-Royals game in the heat and humidity of July in K.C. the following afternoon. (For those keeping track, I attended three major league baseball games in three different cities in the span of seven days—from L.A. to St. Louis to K.C.—and checked two more venues off my Baseball Ballpark Bucket List as well.) A week after flying home from Kansas City, I was in the air again. This time flying to Europe for the planned vacation to Amsterdam and Germany. Traveling requires planning but also a healthy dose of flexibility for the unplanned opportunities that arise.

THERE AND BACK AGAIN

After the week in Europe, a layover in Oakland provided the ideal opportunity of watching an afternoon game (Brewers-A's) and checking stadium #19 off my Ballpark Bucket List. (But wait, there's more!) Only three days after getting home from Amsterdam and Germany, I flew down to San Diego again to visit my dear friend Keisha—whom I'd met in London in 2018. The summer was almost over, and my trip wasn't even planned until we were talking about our summer travels one night. By the end of the conversation, we had decided one more adventure was required to close out the summer in style. (I have continually learned that spontaneity has its benefits. So take the trip and enjoy the adventure and memories created.)

After spending four exceptionally fun and relaxing days in

the sun with Keisha, her three wonderful daughters, and her friends, I was dumping sand out of my Birkenstocks at the airport right before boarding a plane back to Boise. (Whew! Looking back at journals and pictures from that summer it seems crazy to have packed *that* much travel into only a handful of weeks and I loved all of it!) That bustling six-week period of the summer was dizzying at times but so completely worth every last bit of energy, money and time that went into it. Knowing I may not have the opportunity to experience anything like that summer again helped fill my mental scrapbook nearly to capacity.

WE ALL NEED A RESET BUTTON AT TIMES

Traveling to so many locations around America and Europe allowed me to reset my life by reflecting and prioritizing my goals and the people in it. It also taught me to worry less about money and appreciate experiences regardless of how much— or how little—money you have or spend. The cost of things should be judged by the special memories and happiness created, which will last longer than any amount of money will. (A great nugget of advice for life which my friend Paul says often.) Remember, we should measure how happy and fulfilled our experiences make us feel—instead of how much money it costs—when creating our special mental bookmarks along the way.

For many years, I've believed the amount of happiness you have in your life—not the amount of money—equals success. Money doesn't hurt, of course, but you can still be happy without being the wealthiest person around. Having said this, I'd like to try out the "problems" that come with being a millionaire. (Note to publishers: I'm willing to write a book about it, too. Just sayin'.)

GETTING OUT OF OUR COMFORT ZONE

Getting out of our comfort zone—and out of our own way—is essential to moving forward in life and experiencing growth. While it's possible to get out of our comfort zone without traveling, I've found being away from my normal routine gets me out of my zone much more frequently. And by doing so, it has forced me to see things from different perspectives and makes me more comfortable with being uncomfortable. Like most things in life, the more we do something, the easier it becomes. Sometimes getting out of our comfort zone is a choice, and sometimes it isn't. Going through a difficult breakup or divorce—or any challenging life transition—often forces us out of our comfort zone more abruptly than we otherwise might've been.

Since that's the case for many people, embracing the opportunities of pushing the parameters of your comfort zone allows for taking control and ownership of the experiences that will follow. And, even if you don't look back on some of these moments with a smile, you'll likely remember what you learned from getting past your discomfort. I remember feeling like marriage provided comfort, but it also led me to complacency. By expanding my comfort zone, I gained more confidence and understanding of how much more I was capable of experiencing in life than had I remained comfortable and— even more problematic—complacent.

MOVING YOUR PLOT FORWARD

At times, I struggled with pushing my comfort zone parameters after divorce constantly forced me into doing exactly that. My living situation, my career—everything I had grown accustomed to during all those years of marriage—changed drastically. So I was out of my comfort zone often. Life situations often dictate when we experience something new—or just *different* from our usual way of doing things—which provides us with opportunities to grow. Expanding our comfort zones helps us adapt to change, adopt new norms, and become adept at navigating new situations in life. By learning to adapt and roll with the changes, we naturally end up adopting different norms for ourselves, which makes us more adept at continuing to overcome changes in our lives going forward.

Complacency holds us back from understanding this process. In other words, complacency can be comforting, but extremely limiting. Complacency may feel good, but in the long run—if we aren't seeing life from different perspectives and growing from our experiences—we aren't really living life to the fullest. Some people will disagree with this statement, mostly out of their stubborn desire to keep things *as is*, which I understand completely. But from where I'm standing, I am much better off after being forced out of where I'd been sitting in life. (See what I did there? Fortunately, you've almost reached the end of the book and won't be further subjected to these cheeky little quips.) If we truly want to live life to the fullest, being complacent isn't the ideal path to getting there.

Overall, experiencing unprecedented amounts of travel allowed me to enjoy many more people, places and situations than if I'd remained married and complacent. So many people I now count as friends were unknown to me prior to getting divorced. And some of these people will undoubtedly become my lifelong friends. These unexpected friends helped me push my comfort zone boundaries by trying new things. I will be forever grateful to them for doing so.

I've also experienced many new things alone—by my choosing. The cathartic and amazing solo road trip across America brought me to a new appreciation of my freedom and independence. Traveling to Europe in consecutive years was amazing as well and provided additional perspective on my married past and life in general. (Traveling prior to the Covid-19 pandemic was especially fortuitous because most of the trips wouldn't have been possible in 2020 and much of 2021—so I'm glad I went when I could, while I could.)

Saying yes to so many opportunities has yielded countless experiences and mental bookmarks, which have been absolutely integral to my growth process. Again, this was something the earlier version of me would not have been comfortable with. Being single and alone for a good portion of time after Brooke and I ended our incredible travel run taught me how much I could experience by getting out of my comfort zone. And facing my fears of being alone early on—especially on my first solo trip to the Oregon Coast—helped me become emotionally available for future travel adventures, whether solo or with others.

Despite appearances to the contrary, learning to say "yes" in the early months after divorce challenged my old habits of over-analyzing situations and staying in my comfort zone. My first instinct had long been to hesitate until my analytical side had properly processed every angle before accepting—but often rejecting—an idea or opportunity. Looking back at all of these adventures helped me realize how much growth I'd allowed myself to experience when getting out of my own way. Brooke's mentoring and patience as I was processing a difficult life change helped me learn to let go of my past—while also embracing a new future of potential opportunities.

Technically, I had freedom and independence upon divorcing. In reality, though, it took time before I learned that being free and independent could feel as liberating as it eventually would. Initially, I felt overwhelmed by the gravity of being alone and making decisions for myself and no longer for two people. I felt stuck. During my trips with Brooke and others—

but especially when traveling alone—I realized my freedom and independence provided endless possibilities for the present and future.

Each of us is the main character in our own story. Moving our plot forward is one way to no longer feel stuck. All of these experiences and realizations helped me move my plot and story forward and gave me the necessary confidence to leave the past where it belonged. Before long, I started looking ahead for opportunities to spread my wings and fly.

FINDING MY ELIXIR

American author Joseph Campbell wrote *The Hero's Journey* many years ago. At lunch one day, a friend mentioned the concept that each of us takes some form of a hero's journey during our lifetime. From that conversation, the word elixir stuck in my head. The old-fashioned word has various meanings, and we talked about how elixir can represent the solution to a problem. In Campbell's book, he said the elixir may be magical or medicinal and could be used to help others.

For some people, the elixir might be freedom or wisdom gained. For others it could be confidence or love. While discussing the concepts Campbell presented in the book, the overall message that change is possible for *everyone* became obvious. Each of us can—and must—overcome adversity in our lives and get past some of our fears. Naturally, we all deal with adversity and face our fears differently. My friend pointed to all of my post-divorce travels, the people I connected with along the way and finding happiness on my journey as evidence I had indeed found a solution to my problem during all of the years since the divorce.

So what were the problems I was seeking a solution to since becoming a divorcee? After being in my comfort zone and complacent for so many years, I suddenly felt stuck and fearful about facing life alone. Immediately after moving into my own apartment and finding myself lonelier than I'd ever felt in my entire life, my confidence level dropped precipitously. Replaying so many pre-divorce conversations in my head during those painful post-divorce months only sank my confidence further. For so many years my confidence and happiness had been tied directly to my marriage, and I feared a future of being alone. The most significant problem I sought a solution to was wondering if—and when—I'd be happy again.

Initially, saying no to going to places which held memories of my ex-wife kept me in a spin cycle. Not wanting the spin cycle to descend into a downward spiral, I realized saying yes to *myself* was the first step toward facing my fears of being alone. The result of this decision was my determination to take that first solo trip to the Oregon Coast. Campbell would call this action "Crossing the Threshold" because I had faced my fears head on, but I had no idea at the time my journey had any such label. The result of that trek to the sea was learning—slowly at first—I could do these types of trips on my own. I began saying yes to meeting new people, visiting old and new places and creating memories in the process.

I said yes to meeting Brooke and others who would become mentors to me along the way. Saying yes to spontaneous travel opportunities led to beginning unexpected friendships. This led to pursuing my Baseball Ballpark Bucket List, golfing with Lamar in San Diego, flying to Las Vegas in the middle of the night, playing baseball in a cornfield called The Field of Dreams, driving solo across the country from Boston to Boise, living my own Tale of Two Cities by visiting London and Paris, visiting The Netherlands and Germany the following year, standing alone under the twinkling stars in Glacier National Park, then being surrounded by throngs of people in Times

Square while bright lights flashed constantly. All of these people, places and experiences helped me gain a new level of confidence and happiness I hadn't previously felt.

Had I found my life's elixir? If experiencing opportunities fully while gaining knowledge and freedom is the measure of finding my elixir, then yes. In the years since divorce I'd done more living than I had throughout the entire marriage. This realization helped me understand so much more about life and shaped how I approach opportunities moving forward while writing my next chapters. I had evolved from being a single guy who had lost his confidence upon divorce to gaining more confidence the longer I was single—instead of the other way around. Traveling and meeting all of the people who came into my life when—and where—they did was extremely fortuitous and life changing. Learning to say yes broke me out of my comfort zone, which reinforced my gained confidence even more.

Most importantly, learning I am worthy of having a life full of meaningful adventures—with others and on my own—helped me realize I am now better prepared for Act II of my life. My self-worth and regained confidence come from within and are no longer wrapped up in someone else. Overall, I'm better prepared for a relationship and love whenever it comes my way. (I'm still in no hurry though.) At my core, I haven't changed who I am. But I have adapted and gained wisdom throughout all of the experiences—positive and negative—which I've been fortunate to pursue. I am now better equipped to move forward than I previously had been as a married man.

HAPPINESS IS IN THE PURSUIT

Life is the culmination of experiences. And our experiences include many people, places and moments—each to be savored as much as possible if we want to be fully engaged in living. Making efforts to stay more positive than negative on a daily basis is challenging at times but can be extremely rewarding. I've found traveling is a path to being positive and hopeful, even on days when it may be dark and gloomy around you. Providing an escape from the daily grind, traveling tends to allow us to focus on other things because we're not wrapped up in the same issues as in our everyday lives.

I now realize my goals of traveling to iconic locations and seeing games at all of the major league ballparks is only part of the experience. Enjoying and appreciating the journey there—and back again—is more important than any of the destinations I've reached. The people we meet, the places we go and the moments we get to experience become the memories and mental bookmarks we hold onto for the rest of our lives. This is why I travel as much as possible.

All of my travels—whether with family and friends or on my own—have provided a lifetime of wonderful moments. I'm hopeful that many adventures and a future full of creating more incredible memories are ahead of me. Time will tell how many chapters are yet to be written, but I'll be grateful to experience each opportunity as it arises and continue to look back fondly on the times I've enjoyed along the way.

And that's when I found myself finishing one chapter of my life and starting the next...

> *"The secret of happiness is this: let your interests be as wide as possible, and let your reactions to the things and persons that interest you be as far as possible, friendly rather than hostile."*
>
> *- Bertrand Russell*

EXTRA INNINGS

Baseball: More Than Just a Game

As of this writing, I have experienced games at 23 of the 30 MLB ballparks across the United States. Before Covid-19 disrupted all of our lives in March 2020, I had plans to attend four more ballparks that summer. Of course I was disappointed with Covid erasing my plans. But compared to the challenges faced by so many people around the country and the world, canceling my travel plans was easily categorized as a "first world" problem.

Fortunately, I was able to visit four more stadiums—and see six major league games total—in the summer of 2021. I traveled to Arlington/Dallas (via Austin) with my cousin Megan, Brian and Mckenzie for ballpark #19 and a Rays-Rangers game. For Father's Day Weekend, I took a road trip to Seattle for a Rays-Mariners game with my brother Bob and two of my nephews, Mason and Jared. Then flew to New York City and watched the Mets-Yankees on the 4th of July and then Citi Field the next night for a Brewers-Mets game to check off ballparks #20 and #21. In September, I flew to Phoenix and ballpark #22 and enjoyed two Diamondbacks-Dodgers games with my friends Paul and Chad.

In the summer of 2022, I returned to New York City and

took in my first Broadway show—*Into the Woods*—with my new friend Christine, who is a big fan of Broadway shows. We also traveled by train to Philadelphia for ballpark #23, which was the fourth major league game I attended that summer (including two in L.A. with Paul and one in Seattle with Kyle). Each adventure was well worth the wait and made even more memorable because of quality time spent with friends and family.

I continue traveling and being grateful for doing so. Saying yes keeps me from getting complacent in life. Traveling allows me to meet new people, visit different places and learn from new experiences. The reasons for our journeys may change due to unforeseen challenges or circumstances, but I plan to keep traveling when I can, while I can. Ultimately, it has helped me live my life to the fullest and my experiences might help others continue their journey forward as well.

Living all of these memorable stories makes me hope for someone special with whom I can create future mental bookmarks. Eventually, I'd like to find someone who enjoys traveling as much as I do and be able to experience the journey together. There's one main difference between when I started my post-divorce journey and where I am today: I no longer *need* a person to make me happy—many years as a single man have proven that—but remaining single isn't what I *want* for the future chapters of my life. I hope a special someone is out there somewhere. If I don't find her, my life will still be a happy one—and a successful one—because I'm enjoying the journey and not relying on the destination to provide ultimate happiness.

ACKNOWLEDGEMENTS

When I began writing this book in the spring of 2020, I remember thinking how great it would be to become a published author someday. I wanted my book to be entertaining, funny and maybe even inspirational. That's still my hope and I thank all of my readers for taking this journey with me and for being so supportive throughout the process.

At the top of my Thank You List, of course, are my closest family and friends who gave me the base support anyone needs upon divorce and when setting out on the journey of writing a book. I also want to give a very big THANK YOU to all of my past and present students and their parents who have been supportive, inquisitive and encouraging throughout the process. The questions you asked in the halls, in class, at sporting events—and just about anytime we talked—always made me smile and pushed me to continue forward despite the roadblocks life throws at all of us. When you asked questions—How's your book coming? How many chapters have you written so far? What's the title? When will you finally be done?—it showed interest in my project which helped me to stay focused on enjoying the writing process.

The support from all of you motivated me, especially since I knew many of you would be reading it someday. So my BIGGEST thank you definitely goes out to my former students at

Borah High and current students at Boise High. Your genuine interest, positivity and encouragement truly made a difference and words cannot express how much love I have for all of you.

During the process I discovered a taste—and need—for coffee while working on this book. The wonderful, hilarious and kind people I've met at Lucky Perk in Meridian, Flying M in Nampa and Starbucks locations in Boise—especially the Franklin Road and Broadway locations—literally gave me a timely jolt of energy. Your support and encouragement on all of those mornings, afternoons and evenings—typically after a long workday—made me smile and boosted my spirit on many occasions.

Finally, I want to thank my excellent group of editors. Kyle and Alex with Atmosphere Press were friendly, professional and excellent in helping me fine tune my book. To my friend since high school, Mike, your questions and feedback during this past year truly helped me focus on so many aspects of this book which I may have otherwise overlooked. I look forward to celebrating with you the next time you're back in the state. To Shannon (aka "The Corker")—who was involved early in the process—thank you for your perspective, wit and laughter. Thank you, George, for all of our lunchtime book talk sessions. We laughed and bantered about ideas and your input was absolutely integral to the process of completing this book. To my former colleague and English teacher, Stephanie, thank you for helping me fix my grammatical errors so my book reads smoother. And to Christine, an amazing educator and editor, for providing so many insightful points of clarification and perspective which helped my writing tremendously. I couldn't have produced the final version of this book without ALL of your guidance, help and especially humor. I'm very fortunate to count each of you as my friends.

ABOUT ATMOSPHERE PRESS

Atmosphere Press is an independent, full-service publisher for excellent books in all genres and for all audiences. Learn more about what we do at atmospherepress.com.

We encourage you to check out some of Atmosphere's latest releases, which are available at Amazon.com and via order from your local bookstore:

Finding Us, by Kristin Rehkamp

The Ideological and Political System of Banselism, by Royard Halmonet Vantion (Ancheng Wang)

Unconditional: Loving and Losing an Addict, by Lizzy and Adam

Telling Tales and Sharing Secrets, by Jackie Collins, Diana Kinared, and Sally Showalter

Nursing Homes: A Missionary's Journey Through Heaven's Waiting Room, by Tim Eatman Ph.D.

Timeline of Stars, by Joe Adcock

A Boy Who Loved Me, by Wilson Semitti

The Injustice in Justice, by Charmaine Loverin

Living in the Gray, by Katie Weber

Living with Veracity, Dying with Dignity, by Alison Clay-Duboff

Noah's Rejects, by Rob Kagan

A lot of Questions (with no answers)?, by Jordan Neben

Cowboy from Prague: An Immigrant's Pursuit of the American Dream, by Charles Ota Heller

Sleeping Under the Bridge, by Melissa Baker

The Only Prayer I Ever Have to Say Is Thank You, by M. Kaya Hill

Amygdala Blue, by Paul Lomax

A Caregiver's Love Story, by Nancie Wiseman Attwater

ABOUT THE
AUTHOR

SCOTT LOONEY was born and raised in Caldwell, Idaho. As the second-born in a family of six kids, he learned to share, play fair and mediate disagreements at a young age. When not working and traveling, Scott loves hiking, playing tennis, and golfing with friends and family. He has enjoyed many travel opportunities throughout his life—including some involving baseball—and is looking forward to returning to his favorite places. He attended Boise State University and lives in Boise. This is his first published book.